DATE DUE

MR 13'89			

DEMCO

•

Border Fury

•

BORDER FURY

A Picture Postcard Record
of Mexico's Revolution
and U.S. War Preparedness, 1910–1917

• • •

Paul J. Vanderwood
and Frank N. Samponaro

6224

University of New Mexico Press
Albuquerque, New Mexico

Text set in Galliard by the University of
  New Mexico Printing Plant
Design by Barbara Jellow
Printed and bound by BookCrafters, Inc.

Library of Congress Cataloging in Publication Data

Vanderwood, Paul J.
  Border fury.

  Bibliography: p.
  Includes index.
  1. Mexico—History—Revolution, 1910–1920.
2. Postcards—United States—History—20th century.
3. Mexican-American Border Region—History—20th century.
4. United States. Army—History—Punitive Expedition into
Mexico, 1916. I. Samponaro, Frank N., 1940–   . II. Title.
F1234.V2   1987   972.08′1   87-10979
ISBN 0-8263-0990-9

Contents

•

To Marsha and Glenn

•

Introduction

Photographers write history with their cameras, and we are indebted to them for a better understanding and appreciation of our past. Some of their best and most innovative photographic work occurred in the early years of this century and fueled a picture postcard craze that captivated the United States. At the time, innovations in cameras, film, and printing stock made it possible for almost anyone to produce his own personalized picture postcard, and as the fad took hold, thousands and thousands of individuals made and exchanged photo postcards. Images of the daily life of small American villages would have been lost to history had it not been for the photo postcard, as would have been the significant and often spectacular events of the period, such as Mexico's revolution raging along the border and the hasty mobilization of U.S. armed forces sent there to contain the rebellion on foreign territory. Occasionally in rather fuzzy and unimaginative images,

but often in pictures richly steeped in the spontaneity and the luck of an amateur's click, these photos enormously enrich the historical documentation of their times.

To be expected, but crucial to historians, the postcards contained not only photos but messages; in effect, the people who sent them created mini-diaries. When stitched together, their brief writings reveal how the senders felt about themselves and their experiences, or at least what they wanted others to believe about them. Personal comments frequently written on the cards render on-the-spot and at-the-moment details and observations not available elsewhere. No doubt, photo postcards and their messages are a treasure trove for the social historian as well as for specialists whose interests range from architecture to armaments and from dress to transportation. For this book we have mined thousands and thousands of postcards which treat the themes of our study: the Mexican Revolution and U.S. war preparedness along the border from 1910 to 1917.

Our initial interest in the value of picture postcards for historical study derived from a small, personal collection donated by a rancher to the Nita Stewart Haley Memorial Library in Midland, Texas. A member of the staff asked us to evaluate them, less in a monetary than in a historical sense. The photos seemed mildly interesting, nothing more than that. A number had not been seen elsewhere, either published or in collections. We thought maybe they offered material for a book, or maybe not, and decided to proceed cautiously. We did not know it at the time, but the postcard collector's bug had already bitten us.

Some heat for the project was generated in El Paso, where we uncovered a group of cards produced by Walter H. Horne, who turned out to be one of the most fascinating and prolific border-area postcard producers of the period. Then we found some of Horne's personal correspondence in the possession of a real estate developer. We still did not know very much about picture postcards, but we surely recognized the historical value of Horne's correspondence. We saw possibilities in combining those letters with the cards. But the developer sensed a profit in Horne's papers and priced them well beyond our means. Fortunately, he eventually softened toward the El Paso Public Library, which purchased the letters and made them fully available to us for use in this book. Subsequently, we uncovered more Horne correspondence, which we photocopied, used, and then donated the copies to the library.

By now postcard fever had set in, and the frantic search for more cards was on. We located a variety of appropriate materials at public institutions—colleges, libraries, historical societies, archives—and then advertised in the newsletters of postcard dealers and collectors, which immersed us totally in their world.

Who knows why people collect picture postcards. We asked one of the world's recognized, most discerning postcard collectors, Andreas Brown, a New York City appraiser of and dealer in rare books and manuscripts, to explain himself. He took a vigorous stand on the subject; postcard collectors, he said, are different from, say, stamp or coin collectors. Brown finds no intrinsic value in stamp and coin collections; they are the work of individuals with a "checklist mentality." That is, they collect merely to fill prescribed blank spaces in a printed notebook. (Stamp and coin collectors would undoubtedly dispute Brown's contentions.) On the other hand, Brown continued, postcard collectors are students of history; they recover and preserve the past and, at the same time, satisfy their pangs of nostalgia and craving for refuge in much less complicated former times. Indeed, postcard collectors most avidly seek cards which depict scenes of their old hometowns and recall remembrances of their unencumbered youth.

This nostalgia—the search for one's roots, the longing for a simplicity and wholesomeness that seem to have disappeared—has become part of America's mentality, and it has also led to a renaissance in postcard collecting. Cards which cost 25¢ to $1.00 in the early 1970s, then $1.00 to $5.00 later in the decade, now have become a full-blown fad. Interesting and unusual views can now fetch $20.00.

Although we have entered their field, we are not (some say, not yet) postcard collectors. A number of collectors were extraordinarily generous with their cards and loaned them to us with a minimum of restrictions. In some cases their cards were neatly preserved in cellophane holders and loosely indexed in shoeboxes. In others, the cards we sought had disappeared into the indescribable disarray of a collector's intertwined multiple hobbies and interests; some collectors of postcard are irrepressible collectors of anything. They let us dig around in cluttered bookshelves and catch-all cartons where our finds were frequently significant enough to make it worthwhile.

Our search for cards with their messages took us to the U.S. Library of Congress and the National Archives, then from coast to coast to see special collections at university and city libraries, to explore holdings of various historical societies, and to examine personal collections from New York City to Warren, Ohio, to Pebble Beach, California, and even London, England. We went to postcard fairs in San Diego, California, and in London; we hunted in the bookstalls along the Seine in Paris, in the specialty shops under Charing Cross Station in London, among antique dealers off Madrid's Puerta del Sol, and at the infamous flea market, La Lagunilla, in Mexico City. Everywhere we encountered cards of interest, although many were duplicates and others faded, scarred, or mutilated. All in all, we must have reviewed more than 20,000 cards.

To our satisfaction—and, we hope, that of our readers—we prove our point with this book: our knowledge and appreciation of the past would be diminished significantly without these photo postcards and their messages. For example, the cards we used yield more precise information than any other available source on weapons and equipment employed by both the Mexican revolutionaries and the U.S. military during this period. The cards and their messages emphasize the importance of the border experience in experimenting with new equipment and in modernizing and training the U.S. military for future action (meaning wars), an important point largely missed by American historians, even those who have specialized on the period and on such subjects. Observers of war preparedness said it at the time—America had Pancho Villa to thank for bringing the U.S. Army up to par with the nation's ambitions as a world power. This surge of preparedness is witnessed through the postcards.

The jingoistic patriotism of so many soldiers, frustrated by national policies which precluded their outright invasion of Mexico, also is apparent in the cards. These men did not just disparage Mexicans as an enemy; they disdained them as human beings, and the popular literature of the times nourished this bias. Photo images of Germans during World War I, or even Spaniards during the Spanish-American War, were not nearly as sinister or degrading as those of Mexicans during the revolution. Is it likely that the more another people differ in physical appearance, the more likely they are to be caricatured and vilified? Cultural anthropologists can wrestle with that question. Still, their prejudices did not deter American soldiers from deserting to Mexican military contingents, where some received good pay for their technical expertise as machine gunners, artillerymen, dynamiters, and airplane pilots. Others seem to have joined the Mexicans just for the opportunity to engage in a lively fire fight. Desertions for whatever reason to date have merited little attention in border histories of the period, partially because historians have relied more on official military sources than on postcards mailed by ordinary soldiers.

Just how soldiers stationed on the border felt about Mexicans can be inferred by the tremendous number of postcards depicting burned and mutilated Mexican corpses which they sent back home, often with the sentiment: "A good greaser is a dead one." One postcard company printed on its cards: "Types seen along the Mexican Border: The Mexican laborer (peon) is cheap, and it requires many of them to accomplish much, but there are millions to be had. They are happy-go-lucky and are unconcerned for the future."

We might speculate about the role of such postcards in the formation of American public opinion concerning Mexico's revolution and Mexicans themselves. The boys on the border sent these cards everywhere, even overseas. At home, their families proudly passed them on to neighbors; their men were serving Uncle Sam. Batches ended up in scrapbooks on living room tables. In villages and towns, in city neighborhoods, postcards from the border appeared in drugstores and drygoods and hardware shops, wherever people habitually gathered to socialize and to gossip. Picture postcards from the "front" became a center of attention.

While they excited the imagination, the cards also stimulated patriotism at a time when the U.S. was flexing its muscle, even if it did not possess the military bite to back up its bark. Postal images featured the militiamen at a sort of gigantic pep rally along the border. The boys were raring to go over the top into Mexico and on to France. How the cards contributed to the growth of the nationalistic fervor that helped to sweep the country into World War I may be difficult to assess, but the tenor and substance of the pictures, plus the messages written on the cards, certify that picture postcards must have made their contribution to the country's mental set.

In overview, the cards assembled for this book reflect a dramatically changing America. For example, the troops from Kansas are seen riding to the border in covered wagons, but they soon were training among armored cars, airplanes, sophisticated intelligence-gathering equipment, and long-range artillery guns. Frontier days had given way to an expanded and much more modern world.

Millions and millions of photo postcards concerning a seemingly endless variety of themes await serious research and analysis in public repositories and in private hands. We certainly do not mean to say that history can or should be written only from picture postcards, but these cards provide significant insights into our past. Although the professional scholar has largely ignored them, the collector has all along recognized their historical value. We hope to stimulate our colleagues to take a look. We can assure those who use them a fruitful and enjoyable time.

How can we thank all those who have in such good spirits instructed, cajoled, and otherwise impelled and assisted us to complete this book? Persistent encouragement from collectors such as

Andreas Brown in New York City; Carter Rila in Gaithersburg, Maryland; John Hardman of Warren, Ohio; D. J. Sobery of Decatur, Georgia; and Samuel Stark of Pebble Beach, California, was as important as their willingness to permit us to draw upon their immense personal collections for this project. Other collectors too numerous to name here are fully appreciated for contributions which allowed us to fill in pictorial gaps in our storyline and to select cards in the best condition for reproduction. No less kind nor less helpful were the staffs of the many public institutions we approached in our search for postcards: the National Archives of the United States and Library of Congress, special collections in the libraries of the Universities of California, Los Angeles; Arizona; Texas at Austin; and Loyola-Marymount in Los Angeles. Thanks go to the San Diego Historical Society and to the Nita Stewart Haley Memorial Library in Midland, Texas. A very special commendation is due Ms. Mary Sarber, curator of the Southwestern Room at the El Paso Public Library, who not only opened the collection of Walter H. Horne postcards to us but gave us the benefit of her own research on Horne. Equal gratitude goes to Philip L. Condax, director of the Department of Technology, and Andrew H. Eskind, director of Interdepartmental Services, both of the International Museum of Photography at George Eastman House, Rochester, New York. Technical experts at San Diego's Aerospace Center assisted with the identification of military planes, trucks, and other equipment in the photographs. Robert E. McNellis of El Paso, Texas, located additional letters of Horne.

Finally, we relied on good friends and colleagues to weed out mistakes and to clarify our writing. Dr. Rosalie Schwartz of San Diego, a technical editor and Ph.D. in Latin American history, did her best to blend our quite different writing styles into one and gave the manuscript a tough, final editing. Her endeavor is especially appreciated. Professor George Miller of the University of Delaware, who has done original work on postcard history, and Professor Oscar J. Martínez, director of Latin American Studies at the University of Texas, El Paso, who has written well and widely on border history, also reviewed the manuscript and offered helpful advice. Carolyn and Charles Roy, both Latin American specialists, read the manuscript for grammatical flaws. All of these individuals helped to make this book a much better one, and we thoroughly appreciate their contributions. Any errors and fog that remain are our responsibility.

Paul J. Vanderwood
    San Diego State University
Frank N. Samponaro
    University of Texas of the Permian Basin

Chapter One

The Picture Postcard Craze and Mexico's Revolution

The sequence of events that produced a frenzied interest in collecting picture postcards in the United States by the middle of the first decade of the twentieth century began many years earlier in Europe, where the first postal card was produced. To the uninitiated, the distinction between a postal card and a postcard may appear inconsequential, but collectors and historians recognize its significance. The older postal card is issued by government postal authorities and sold prestamped. Its purpose is strictly utilitarian. The privately manufactured postcard requires that the correct postage be affixed at the time of mailing and is often imaginative as well as useful. What we today call postcards have in the past been referred to as souvenir cards, private mailing cards, and view cards. The words *post card* only became legal in the United States by virtue of postal regulations issued in 1901.[1]

The Austro-Hungarian Empire issued the first postal card on October 1, 1869, stamped with the likeness of Emperor Francis Joseph I. A young Austrian professor, Dr. Emanuel Hermann, borrowed the concept from Dr. Heinrich von Stephen of the Germanic Postal Union.[2] The postals won immediate popularity because people found them cheaper and more convenient than letters for brief personal and business messages. Within a few years most European countries followed the Hapsburg Empire and produced their own postal cards.

The United States Congress also recognized the potential of the new form of communication and on May 1, 1873 authorized the Post Office Department to begin issuing postal cards to postmasters throughout the nation. The cards were sold for a penny each to facilitate short printed or written communication that met the needs of business and social life.[3] Americans loved the postals as much as Europeans; within six months, sixty million cards had been purchased.[4]

Wily entrepreneurs on both sides of the Atlantic assessed this popularity and concluded correctly that good money could be made producing their own cards—with pictures on the front. The earliest surviving example of this important new genre is the work of August Schwartz, a German printer whose woodcut scene from the Franco-Prussian War adorned cards that were purchased by soldiers and mailed home.[5] Other German postcards of the same period pictured resorts, hotels, and restaurants in one corner, but there were also holiday greeting cards, sentimental postcards, and ones with patriotic themes. Once whetted, the European appetite for pictorial cards grew rapidly, and steadily increasing numbers were manufactured and sold. By the 1890s collecting postcards had become a popular hobby. The appearance on drawing room tables of special albums in which postcards could be conveniently viewed and preserved became quite fashionable. Even Britain's Queen Victoria was an avid collector.[6]

Where the Europeans led, the Americans soon followed with their own special enthusiasm. Publishers in the United States began printing holiday greetings and advertisements on the backs of government postals in the 1870s.[7] But privately produced picture postcards did not come into general use until 1893, when thousands were sold as souvenirs of the World's Columbian Exposition in Chicago. These postcards and others published privately before the landmark congressional legislation of May 19, 1898 are called "pioneer cards." Most peo-

ple bought them as souvenirs of a visit to some city or resort. With interest in view cards still relatively new, sales remained limited. No large publishers yet marketed the product on a national or even on a regional scale.[8]

The 1898 postal law boosted the popularity of view cards because it granted them the same mailing privileges as government-issued postals. The legislation cut the two-cent fee for mailing privately manufactured postcards by half and required that the postcards have approximately the same physical characteristics as government postals and contain the phrase *Private Mailing Card-Authorized by Act of Congress, May 19, 1898.*[9] After December 24, 1901, newly revised postal regulations gave manufacturers the option of omitting that rather cumbersome phrase as long as they printed the words *Post Card* in its place.[10]

The reduced mailing cost was only one factor in the meteoric nationwide increase in demand for picture postcards by the middle of the first decade of the new century. The post office also began rural free mail delivery for farmers who petitioned their congressmen for the service. Before the advent of the R.F.D. system, free home mail delivery had been available only to approximately 25 percent of the population, those living in towns of at least ten thousand people. Farmers and others who did not qualify for the service had to go for their mail to the nearest post office, often many miles from home. The delivery system for small town and rural America took several years to complete, but by 1906 most of the routes had been established, and isolated homes and farms across the country received mail on a daily basis. The change affected vast numbers of people. In 1900 the Census Bureau classified 60.3 percent of the population as rural, or not living in communities of at least 2,500 inhabitants. The total farm population stood at 29,875,000. While rural Americans accounted for only 54.3 percent of a growing national population in 1910, the number of people living on farms actually increased to 32,077,000.[11]

Daily delivery encouraged new and different uses for mail service that brought the world a little closer. Rural daily newspapers increased in numbers and enjoyed a large growth in circulation. At the same time, Americans living outside of cities and large towns began to send and receive many more picture postcards.[12] Postcards announced a birth or a wedding or invited friends to Sunday dinner. They were cheaper to send than letters and much less expensive than phone calls, that is, if one had access to a telephone. In an era when few people traveled very far from home and few small town newspapers carried news photographs, buying a postcard depicting an event of local, national, or even international interest was a special and affordable treat, for oneself or to send to someone else.

The easy availability of postcards picturing a wide range of subjects stimulated interest in collecting as well as mailing them. Because collecting postcards had become extremely popular in Europe by 1900, several big firms turned them out to meet the demand. European manufacturers, particularly the Germans, produced high-quality lithographic cards in large volume before any comparable American firms came into existence. As a result, German manufacturers captured a major part of the American market at the beginning of the postcard era. They established efficient networks of wholesalers and jobbers throughout the United States to handle their diverse lines of view cards and retained a large market share until the outbreak of World War I.[13]

Despite the Germans' initial competitive advantage, demand for postcards in America expanded so rapidly that new domestic companies won a substantial share of the market. By 1905 a number of large American manufacturers sold their products nationally, and even more medium-size manufacturers did business on a regional basis. Like the big German companies, these concerns made printed postcards in relatively large quantities. To make printed or photochemically reproduced cards by the processes of photoengraving, photogravure, collotype, or photolithography required a substantial capital outlay to equip a print shop, but once the necessary investment had been made, large numbers of postcards could be turned out at a small cost per unit. For example, halftone images made from photographs were printed on large sheets with postcard backs. Then each imprinted sheet was cut by machine into twenty or thirty individual postcards, depending on size.[14] Firms using these mass production techniques, whether foreign or domestic, acquired a dominant position in the growing market for postcards.

Still, the large manufacturers did not monopolize the market; ample opportunity existed for the small entrepreneur. Thanks to George Eastman, one of the authentic geniuses of the Industrial Revolution in the United States, an individual could go into the postcard business on a shoestring. Many relatively inexpensive cameras began to appear on the American market in the 1880s. The one that soon became by far the biggest seller was invented and manufactured by Eastman and put on sale for the first time in 1888. Eastman called his product the Kodak, a name which he coined himself because he thought it short, pronounceable in any language, distinctive, and easily remembered. The original Kodak box camera measured three and one-half, by three and three-quarters, by six and one-half inches and cost twenty-five dollars, including film and processing. It had a fixed-focus lens of 57 millimeters focal length and an aperture of f/9. A new Kodak came with enough factory-loaded film to take one hundred pictures. After shooting the initial roll of film, the photographer sent the camera back to the manufacturer in Rochester, New York, where the film was removed and developed. The prints were returned to the owner with the camera, which for an additional ten dollars was reloaded with fresh film. With his motto "You press the button, we do the rest," Eastman made amateur photographers out of hundreds of thousands of Americans by the 1890s.[15]

George Eastman's enormously creative mind continued to churn out ideas. Within the first few years of the new century his technological and marketing advances made it possible for individuals of modest means to make their own photographic postcards. By 1899 he had refined the technique for developing film to the point that interested amateurs easily processed their exposures in their own home darkrooms. In 1902 the Eastman Kodak Company capitalized on the emerging postcard fad by issuing postcard-size photographic paper on which images could be printed directly from negatives as easily as on regular paper. But the most dramatic step fol-

lowed in 1903: the Kodak 3A camera swept the market. The new $2.00 camera put photography within the reach of virtually every American. The folding bellows camera, equipped with an f/6.8 lens, had a top shutter speed of one one-hundredth of a second. Its 122-millimeter film had a speed equivalent to an ASA value of about nine, and the negatives were exactly the right dimensions to make postcard-size contact prints (three and one-quarter by five and one-half inches).[16]

Because Eastman's innovations made possible the low-cost production of what collectors today call real photo or photographic postcards, several manufacturers began to market contact printing paper with preimprinted postcard backs. Not surprisingly, the Eastman Kodak Company's Velox and Azo brands emerged as the biggest sellers, but the Defender Photo Supply Company's Argo, Ansco's Cyko, and the Artura Paper Company's Artura all captured significant shares of the market.[17]

The ever-resourceful Eastman devised yet another way to enhance his firm's profits. In 1906 Eastman Kodak offered to print on postcard-backed paper the rolls of film sent to Rochester for processing. Soon parents were mailing postcards to all the relatives with pictures of the children. Of course, one still could go to the local professional photographer's studio to have a family portrait made in postcard format, but if one were so inclined, it was a simple matter to take one's own pictures and send them off to the Kodak plant to be made into postcards.[18]

Americans were manufacturing, buying, mailing, and collecting picture postcards in huge quantities by 1907, when Congress passed postal

Figure 1. An early model of the Kodak 3A. Ease of operation as well as low price accounted for the immediate popularity of this camera. A novice could learn to load and unload the 3A and take pictures with it in only a few minutes. (Photograph by Frank N. Samponaro.)

legislation that further intensified the craze. Before March 1 of that year, the U.S. Post Office Department required that any messages on cards be written on the picture side, often defacing the picture itself. Only the address was permitted on the undivided back. After March 1, however, postcards with divided backs became legal, and cards with the message written on the left side and the address on the right could be mailed.[19] The fact that it became possible to write more than the briefest of messages on picture postcards made them more popular than ever.

By the time the divided-back card appeared, producers of real photo cards had already found an important niche in the rapidly expanding picture postcard business. Small town portrait photographers sought to supplement their incomes by selling view cards with scenes of their towns and villages in the local drugstore.[20] Other individuals, attempting to better themselves financially, went to work with their cameras on a part-time basis. When anything unusual happened—a flood, a fire, a hanging, the visit of a circus—they appeared to record the event with their cameras. They immediately printed their negatives on postcard stock and sold their work to anyone who wanted an "instant" photographic record of the event to keep or to mail to someone else. Since the local newspaper did not print pictures and the larger postcard manufacturers scorned views of purely local interest and limited sales potential, small postcard producers played an important role in capturing America on film during the first and second decades of the twentieth century.[21]

A few small postcard makers with exceptional entrepreneurial skills and the luck to be working in locations where major news events occurred managed to sell substantial numbers of cards and make very good money. Most sold relatively few postcards and earned only modest incomes from their businesses. Nevertheless, several thousand of them lived and worked in communities throughout the nation by 1910, when George Eastman manufactured a product especially tailored to their needs. The new piece of equipment was a printing box designed for 122-millimeter film and made by the Rochester Optical Company (an Eastman Kodak subsidiary) specifically to produce postcards. The *Kodak Trade Journal* of May 1910 announced, "The R.O.C. Post Card Printer is made for the man who desires an inexpensive, yet rapid and trustworthy machine for printing developing-out post cards." The postcard-backed contact printing paper fitted into place against the negative and a small hand lever closed the frame. With exposure completed, the same lever opened the frame and the postcard emerged ready for the developing, stop bath, fixer, washing, and drying stages of the processing cycle. The printer sold for $7.50, but with a generous 40 percent discount for professional photographers. Eastman knew his marketing. Once he sold his printer, he gained steady customers for Kodak postcard-backed paper and processing chemicals.[22]

Whether made by small, one-person operations producing photographic cards or by medium-size and large manufacturers turning out printed ones, the picture postcard business grew at a rapidly accelerating pace after 1905. Sales soon reached immense proportions. Official post office figures for the fiscal year ending June 30, 1908 put the number of cards handled by the department at 667,777,798. By

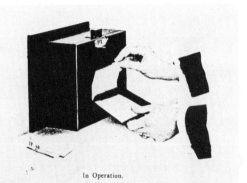

In Operation.

THE R. O. C. POST CARD PRINTER.

The R. O. C. Post Card Printer is made for the man who desires an inexpensive, yet rapid and trustworthy machine for printing developing-out post cards.

The R. O. C. Post Card Printer may be used with either artificial or daylight, but the use of artificial light is recommended owing to its greater uniformity.

The operation of the R. O. C. Post Card Printer is similar to that of an ordinary hand-printing press, as shown in the accompanying illustration. Drop the card into place against the negative, close the frame by means of the small hand lever; at the expiration of the exposure pull back on the lever, which opens the frame and drops the exposed card. The action of closing the frame automatically opens the exposed shutter, and opening the frame closes it. Every mechanical feature is positive in action, and practically impossible to get out of order.

The negative is placed in position by removing the front

Showing Interior Construction With Shutter Partly Opened.

of the printer, and lifting out the spring retained back as shown in the illustration page 8. The printing opening is made full cabinet size, and a cut-out is furnished for post card size,

Figure 2. Advertisement for the Rochester Optical Company postcard printer in the *Kodak Trade Journal*, May 1910.

1913 that total increased to 968 million.[23] Frantic public demand for picture postcards encouraged retailers to put them everywhere: bookstores, drugstores, hotels, department stores, and cigar stands. Pushcart vendors sold them. Shops specialized in postcards, and racks filled with them stood on street corners in most cities and larger towns. Merchants eagerly purchased frames of various designs to organize as many cards as possible in eye-catching displays. Some of the earliest vending machines were made to sell postcards. Enthusiasts established clubs throughout the United States to promote "philocarty" or "cartephilia," as they termed postcard collecting. Manufacturers of cards and other firms enticed collectors with albums in a variety of sizes with precut slots to hold postcards.[24]

Some observers have argued that postcards changed the writing habits of the American people.[25] The long, descriptive phrases and lengthy expressions of endearment that had been common in letter writing gave way to the few terse phrases or sentences required for postcards. Brevity seemed in harmony with a people increasingly in a hurry to keep up with a rapidly changing world. One contemporary pundit lamented, tongue-in-cheek, that the art of letter-writing was being threatened with extinction. He wrote:

Like the heaven-sent relief, the souvenir postal card has come to the man of few ideas and a torpid vocabulary. . . . From jails they carry appeals for bail to faithful friends. The traveler marks his trail as if with confetti by hastily scribbled notes consisting of "Wish you were here, All well." "This is so beautiful. All well." When mother decides that she will stay all night with her daughter in the next town, she sends word home to the family on a souvenir card of the Carnegie Library. When father's dry goods store burns down, he photographs the catastrophe, prints a souvenir card from it and requests the insurance adjuster to drop into town immediately. . . . Baby's arrival, his first tooth, his first trousers, his first bicycle, his first girl, and his first baby all go to the family circle by souvenir postal, for anyone with a camera can make a card these days.[26]

Picture postcards had their heyday in the decade preceding World War I, when a variety of commercially produced cards sold well. Cards commemorated major regional expositions of industry and commerce, as well as less important local conventions and festivals. Advertising cards stimulated sales of a wide range of products and services. Postcards promoted politicians running for elective office and marked important achievements in their careers. While some cards contained views of the major armed conflicts around the world, others showed the signing of peace treaties ending them. Postcards provided a glimpse of the women's suffrage crusade and documented many major and minor news stories. Cards followed the expedition of Commodore Robert E. Perry to the North Pole and the completion of the Panama Canal; they chronicled the opening of county fairs and even small town bowling alleys. Postcards showed common people at work and recorded their leisure time spent at social gatherings, sporting events, parties, and fraternal clubs. There were comic cards and ones with pictures of pretty girls, American presidents, state capitols, trains, ships, dogs, and cats. Some manufacturers made postcards with blatantly racist caricatures of minority groups; others issued ones with macabre scenes like hangings. Cards with views of important landmarks in cities and towns and at resorts always sold well. While spectacular natural or man-made disasters often provided a quick profit for card manufacturers, patriotic and holiday greeting cards remained staples of the business.[27]

Despite this enormous popularity, public interest in picture postcards eventually declined. The Payne-Aldrich Tariff Act of 1909 heralded the end of the postcard era. Large American manufacturers of printed cards argued that protection was necessary for the survival of their industry because of the higher wages paid to American workers. As a result of their lobbying efforts in Washington, the new tariff law significantly increased the duty on imported postcards. On the eve of the effective date of the legislation, most major American importers of German postcards took what appeared to be a prudent step and began to stockpile large quantities of cards, but this action proved to be a serious miscalculation. The postcard supply line became dangerously overloaded; importers provided jobbers with more cards than they could sell to retailers, and retailers became seriously overstocked, some with a full year's supply of cards. Price-cutting began in an effort to reduce inventory. By 1913 one American postcard publisher advertised two million view cards at one-half their production cost. In the increasingly cut-throat environment, fifty large and medium-size postcard manufacturers ceased production in 1913, when the glut of cards plunged prices to the all-time low of five cents a dozen on retail racks. By 1914 the prospects for the recovery of the business appeared so bleak that the National Association of Post Card Manufacturers cancelled that year's convention for lack of interest.[28]

With the domestic printed postcard industry still reeling from the unanticipated repercussions of the Payne-Aldrich Tariff, the outbreak of World War I in 1914 resulted in the almost complete cessation of imports of the German dyes and lithographing equipment that many American firms used to produce printed postcards. The disruption of the supply link from Germany further weakened an already depressed industry.[29] Most important of all, however, the enthusiasm of Americans for picture postcards waned, and they bought fewer of them. Like other fads, the craze for postcards was temporary. Albums that formerly enjoyed a place of prominence on the living room coffee table were consigned to the attic. Postcards no longer served so well the wide number of purposes they once had. Technological innovations were changing people's lifestyles. More of them had telephones and lived in urban areas with access to newspapers printing at least some news photographs. Residents of cities and large towns also had the opportunity to see moving pictures, including newsreels, on a regular basis. People living in rural areas became less isolated as paved roads made travel by automobile more common. All of these factors combined to bring about a substantial decline in postcard sales. Although this decline began gradually, by 1915 the golden age of the picture postcard in the United States had passed.[30]

At least one notable exception countered the decreasing interest in postcards. Sales of cards with views of the Mexican Revolution and of the American military response to Mexico's struggle continued to grow even after 1915. Graphic violence of the revolution occurred close to the United States border. Colorful, swashbuckling revolutionary leaders and U.S. forces, deployed along the frontier and even ordered into combat in Mexico, fascinated the public as they appeared on a virtually limitless number of extraordinarily dramatic and unusually marketable postcards. The demand for cards picturing the Mexican Revolution began in late 1910 and rose until it reached its peak in 1916. Although interest in the postcards waxed and waned, reflecting the intensity of interest in events related to the revolution, the general trend moved steadily upward. When a postcard photographer captured a truly spectacular incident, sales of view cards rose sharply. This pattern was, as might be expected, most pronounced when the incident directly involved Americans.

Although the Mexican Revolution dates officially from 1910, discontent with the government of President Porfirio Díaz had been smoldering for years. A rash of violent labor disturbances, for example, started in June 1906 with the strike at the Consolidated Copper Mining Company in Cananea, Sonora. An extremely rare series of twenty undivided-back postcards depicts incidents that took place during the Cananea strike, which resulted in the loss of twenty-three Mexican and American lives. On one card the unknown photographer has provided posterity with a remarkably clear shot of Colonel W. C. Greene, the American mine manager, addressing a crowd of his restless Mexican workers. The Cananea postcards were the forerunners of hundreds of thousands of cards that recorded the border's history over the next decade.

Following the outbreak of full-scale rebellion against Díaz, picture postcards of the violence in Mexico and of the leading revolutionary personalities became increasingly common in the United States. The initial cards included rather unimaginative and staid portraits of General Díaz and the leader of the insurrection against him, Francisco I. Madero, but postcard photographers soon located some real action. The first noteworthy battle of the revolution along the United States–Mexican frontier took place at Agua Prieta, Sonora, in April 1911. Just across the border the residents of Douglas, Arizona, stood on the roofs of their homes and watched the fighting through binoculars. The following month, El Pasoans discovered that they were in an ideal location to view the combat raging in Ciudad Juárez, Chihuahua. During and immediately following both battles, obscure local photographers crossed the international boundary and recorded on film the fighting, the bodies of the dead, and the badly damaged buildings. These entrepreneurs then made and sold real photo postcards to a public anxious to have a souvenir of the carnage and destruction in Mexico. This first flurry of sales convinced many photographers that such events, particularly the more violent ones, could make the postcard business quite profitable, and as the revolution intensified, they began to turn out postcards in towns all along the border.

By the spring of 1911 increasing numbers of Americans had become aware of the major uprising in progress in Mexico and learned the names of the prominent military chieftains. Some were even willing to spend an occasional nickel to get a glimpse of the military action across the border or to find out what Pancho Villa really looked like. Sales increased steadily in the period through the battles of Ojinaga and Ciudad Juárez in 1913, but the market for Mexican Revolution postcards remained limited primarily to border areas. Small-scale local photographers filled most of the still modest demand; the larger producers of printed cards did not yet consider public interest in the revolution to be great enough to make a major commitment in the national market.

This situation changed dramatically in April 1914 when American sailors and marines, acting on the orders of President Woodrow Wilson, invaded and occupied the city of Veracruz. Banner headlines in newspapers across the United States announced the assault on the Mexican port, and news stories carried details of the fighting and the casualties. Major postcard manufacturers immediately took advantage of the average American's desire to see for himself what was going on in Veracruz. The W. M. Prilay Post Card Company hurried into production with three "Mexican War Series" of cards featuring the U.S. armed forces. Another large postcard publishing concern, the Max Stein Company of Chicago, was soon selling images of the action in Veracruz. Tichnor Brothers, Incorporated, of Boston rapidly followed suit.

Despite the serious interest of large manufacturers in Veracruz, the landing there offered the small postcard producer plenty of opportunity as well. Charles C. C. Cushing of Brooklyn found a market for cards imprinted with a poem entitled "In

Memorium. Vera Cruz," in honor of the American servicemen who had fallen in combat. Among the most interesting postcards depicting the American military operation in Veracruz were the U.S.S. *New Jersey*'s landing batallion cards. They were taken by the ship's photographers, two sailors named Cruse and Shaw, between April 22 and April 30, 1914 and processed in the dark-room on board ship to be sold to crew members at a nominal sum. These cards, like those made for the men of other ships involved in the same operation, were produced exclusively for the crew and were not intended for commercial sale. On a postcard that a young ensign on the *New Jersey*, George W. Hewlett, sent home to Connecticut, he proudly identified his fellow junior officers who also participated in the landing. Hewlett told his family, "This picture was taken on the lot of the filtration plant. My company at this time were in sand hills outpost."[31] While Hewlett did not reveal his feelings about being in Veracruz, a card dated October 21, 1914 and mailed by an unknown serviceman along with others in an envelope to "Miss Annie B," did: "And we get more pay than we get in the States, so that is a little inducement to want to stay here, and to tell the truth I do believe I like it here."[32]

After the Americans withdrew from Veracruz in November 1914, public interest in Mexican affairs declined temporarily as did the sale of postcards. Although a good, steady market continued for cards picturing the revolution, no boom in sales developed in 1915 comparable to the demand of 1914. That would change in 1916 when events of the Mexican Revolution directly involved the United States. On March 9, 1916 forces acting

Figure 3. Formal portraits of postcard photographers are extremely rare. Lee Passmore, a flamboyant San Diego professional, used this postcard for advertising purposes. It shows him standing beside the Circuit camera that he used to photograph panoramic scenes. On the back of the card is his slogan: "You may pass more photographers but none more like Passmore." For some time after he began his career in commercial photography in 1909, Passmore continued to work part time as a guide on a sightseeing boat that operated out of San Diego harbor. Although he did a lively business turning out postcards of troops stationed on the California–Baja California border during the Mexican Revolution, he concentrated on scenic, panoramic prints. Later in life he became famous as a naturalist photographer, specializing in insects. (Courtesy San Diego Historical Society—Ticor Collection.)

under the orders of Mexican rebel leader Pancho Villa raided Columbus, New Mexico, killing seventeen American soldiers and civilians. By March 15, the lead elements of a force of more than twelve thousand United States Army regulars under the command of General John J. Pershing had crossed the border with orders to mount a "punitive expedition" into Mexico.

Then on May 5, Mexican Villista "bandits" raided Glenn Springs and Boquillas, Texas. Two days later President Wilson ordered a partial mobilization of the National Guard; a total of 5,260 officers and men from units in Texas, New Mexico, and Arizona answered the call to active service. Wilson assessed the situation and concluded that these guardsmen and the regular troops already on duty

The Picture Postcard Craze and Mexico's Revolution • 11

were insufficient in number to protect the long border from attack by forces loyal to Villa and Venustiano Carranza, rivals for leadership of Mexico's Revolution. On June 18, he ordered the mobilization of the National Guards of the remaining states to implement his policy of "watchful waiting." By early September nearly 200,000 guardsmen and regulars were on active duty at strategic points from Texas to California. Forty thousand troops camped in the El Paso region alone—the largest concentration of American military personnel in a single area since the Civil War.[33]

The Columbus raid, the Punitive Expedition, and the subsequent mobilization of large numbers of National Guard troops led to an enormous growth in postcard sales. Two principal sources created this demand. For one, people all over the United States suddenly became captivated by affairs on both sides of the border, and postcards breathed life into the events there. But the most intense demand came from the 184,000 National Guard troops on duty in camps from Brownsville, Texas, to San Diego, California.

Contrary to what many guardsmen expected when they left home with their units, they never entered the actual combat. No general order moved them to march south into Mexico, nor did occasional border skirmishes escalate into full-fledged battle. The men drilled and dug trenches and became increasingly bored and disgruntled; most had plenty of time on their hands and at least some money to spend. Very few could not afford the price of a picture postcard to give loved ones and acquaintances a first-hand look at life along the border. A soldier had no trouble buying a card to prove to folks at home that he was at least near the action. Postcards available in YMCAs and post exchanges at camps and in stores and on street corner racks in nearby towns showed scenes of the fighting in Mexico.[34] A guardsman named Roy, stationed near Douglas, Arizona, sent home a card with a picture of Mexicans killed in an unknown battle and asked bluntly: "How do you like this?"[35] Another on duty in San Benito, Texas, mailed a view of what were supposed to be "Typical Mexican Soldiers" to his mother in Sioux Falls, South Dakota, and inquired plaintively: "Why don't you write to me. I haven't heard from you or dad in a coon's age."[36] Cards catalogued the exotic plants and reptiles of the Southwest so a soldier could impress his sweetheart in the North. Lonie, assigned to Camp Leon Springs, Texas, sent his girl friend, Cornelia Hiscock, in Syracuse, New York, a postcard picture of a small rattlesnake and told her: "If you would like one of these just let me know and I will bring one Xmas."[37]

Most guardsmen stationed near the border in 1916 loved to buy and send home cards made by enterprising local photographers showing themselves and their buddies on duty or during their free moments at the camps. But an occasional soldier with a camera acted as his own photographer. One of them wrote on the back of a postcard that he mailed to his family: "All of the boys marked is in my squad. I took the picture but will send some of the whole bunch soon. . . ."[38]

Among the most unique and charming cards mailed during the military buildup were those of Mineral Wells, Texas, guardsman Jodie P. Harris, assigned to duty in the Big Bend country of Texas.

Harris drew cartoons on the backs of penny postal cards and sent them to the drugstore in Mineral Wells for everyone to see. His hand-drawn bored, homesick enlisted men, with no fighting to do, reluctantly carry out make-work tasks assigned to them by their officers. One of his cards complains:

> The border raid, that called out the militia
> Was American made, and sounds mighty fishie,
> No bandits now in sight, why should we fear?
> There is no one to fight, but still we are
> HERE.[39]

With large potential profits from sales to troops along the border and civilians throughout the United States, at least one hundred firms and individuals produced postcards related to the Mexican Revolution by the summer of 1916.[40] Those in the business included the owners of tiny, one-person operations in little towns near the smaller National Guard camps, some of them working only part time with inexpensive photographic equipment to turn out a mere handful of cards. At the opposite pole, large manufacturers, like the International Film Service and the Max Stein Company, made postcards by the hundreds of thousands. In between were the medium-size concerns like the Mexican War Photo Postcard Company and Kavanaugh's War Postals. The market for what the trade referred to as Mexican War postcards reached its peak during 1916, as indicated by the sales figures of Walter H. Horne of El Paso. Horne, who previously had manufactured and sold only a moderate number of photographic cards, proudly informed his mother and brother in a letter on March 21 that his postcard output that day reached 2,700.[41] Only a short time earlier he would

Figure 4. Even the Communists endorsed the idea of the self-made picture postcard and encouraged people to get into the business. Why make money for the capitalists when you can pile it up for yourself? This advertisement appeared in the July 1914 edition of *The Masses*.

have regarded that total as astronomical; however, by early August he could report a daily production rate of 5,000 cards.[42]

During the boom days of 1916 a wide variety of Mexican War postcards sold well. Besides the photographic cards made by small and medium-size producers and the printed cards turned out by their larger rivals, cards with poems on them allowed inarticulate guardsmen to convey to loved ones their feelings about their experiences on the border or about being so far from home on Thanksgiving.

Cards with obviously posed "action" shots proved popular, and scenes photographed some time previously (even during another war) were reprinted, often with a new caption. A big favorite was the reissue of a postcard with a portrait of the notorious Pancho Villa on horseback, now entitled "Gen Francisco Villa the cause of it all." Cards showing the regular army troops of the Pershing expedition on the march in Mexico sold well, as did those purporting to depict the way Mexican people lived. At a time when postcard photographers lacked adequate copyright protection, some card makers pirated potentially popular images.[43] On some occasions a publisher tried to hide the fact that he borrowed someone else's work by touching up his copy negative to remove people, trees, or buildings. On others he substituted a new caption, but often he did neither.

Although postcards with pictures related to the Mexican Revolution sold at record levels in the summer and fall of 1916, a sharp decline in demand occurred by the end of the year. Not only did Americans grow tired of what seemed to be General Pershing's futile pursuit of Villa, but it also appeared that the National Guard forces on the border served no useful purpose. Meanwhile, the ominous situation in Europe drew public attention away from Mexico. President Wilson, concerned about the possibility of war with Germany, ordered Pershing to begin withdrawing his troops from Mexico no later than January 31, 1917. By the end of the first week in February, nearly all the forces participating in the Punitive Expedition were back in the United States.[44] Simultaneously the demobilization of National Guard units on duty in the Southwest began, and by April 6, when the United States declared war on the Central powers, a large majority of the guardsmen had returned home.[45] The intense preoccupation of the American people with events in Europe after the formal declaration of war eclipsed public interest in anything having to do with the Mexican Revolution, including postcards.

Moreover, the rebellion and the U.S. diplomatic wrangling with Mexico that accompanied it moved toward an uneasy conclusion. Neither the fighting nor the verbal maneuvers stopped, but both diminished decidedly. Their decline meant that the dramatic pictorial possibilities—the kind craved by the American public and eagerly exploited by the postcard producers—all but disappeared. Singularly striking events, such as the assassination of Pancho Villa in 1923, still attracted the attention of postcard buyers, but the boom days of 1916 were definitely over. Although the fad ended, the postcards themselves remain to provide collectors, scholars, and interested readers with an invaluable record of the era.

Postcards picturing the violent strike of June 1906 at the Consolidated Copper Mining Company in Cananea, Sonora (just below the Arizona border) greatly stimulated U.S. public interest in Mexican affairs. Among the series of twenty "undivided back" postcards of the events at Cananea, this one taken near the conclusion of the labor disturbance shows Colonel William C. Greene, the American manager of the mine, backed up by a group of rifle-toting gringos, laying down the law to his Mexican employees. (Courtesy U.S. National Archives.)

C. Gral Porfirio Diaz, Presidente de los Estados Unidos Mexicanos.
J. K. I. México.
Regist.

F T
MADERO
HERIDO EN
LA BATALLA
DE CASAS
GRANDES
EL 6 DE
MARZO
1911

This official portrait of General Porfirio Díaz in full dress uniform appeared as a postcard in the United States in 1911 and indicates the awakening interest of the American postcard industry and public toward the Mexican Revolution. At the time, most Americans presumed that the aging dictator would have little difficulty suppressing the rebellion against his regime. (Courtesy El Paso Public Library.)

A Mexican photographer took this picture of the leader of the revolution, Francisco I. Madero, his right arm in a sling as a result of a bullet wound received during the battle of Casas Grandes, Chihuahua, on March 6, 1911. An enterprising photographer, Walter H. Horne of El Paso, reissued the image in postcard format immediately after the assassination of Madero in 1913. (Courtesy John Hardman Collection.)

AFTER THE BATTLE OF APR, 13, AGUA PRIETA, MEXICO,

The first significant combat between Mexican federal troops and rebel forces along the border occurred at Agua Prieta, Sonora, in April 1911. Scores of amateur "Kodak fiends" crossed the line from Douglas, Arizona, after the battle to take pictures. They were accompanied by a few professional photographers who turned their negatives into postcards and put them on sale. This card shows two Americans, a few rebels, and some Mexican civilians viewing the remains of victims of the fighting. It was among the first of thousands of postcards sold in the United States over the next several years that depicted graphic scenes of death and destruction along the border. (Courtesy Arizona Historical Society.)

The first battle of Ciudad Juárez in May 1911 attracted the avid and lurid interest of many El Paso residents. While some viewed the combat from the comparative safety of roof tops, others wanted a closer look. Despite Mayor Charles E. Kelly's warning that Mauser bullets would "rain on the banks of the Rio Grande," downtown streets had to be roped off to limit the number of sightseers on the river front. (Courtesy El Paso Public Library.)

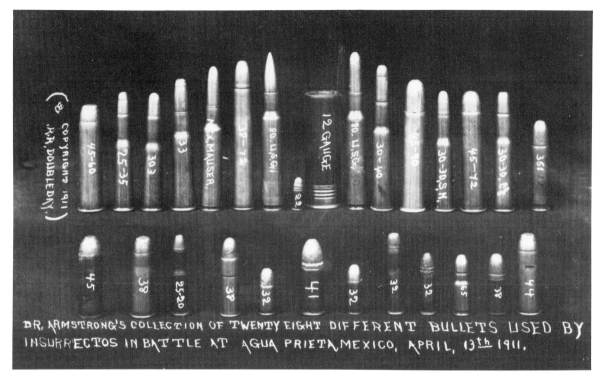

In an attempt to discourage the pirating of his photographic work, R. R. Doubleday of Douglas, Arizona, carefully wrote "copyright 1911" on his negative before printing postcards from it. Such efforts, however, were normally futile. Some publishers simply obliterated the names of original photographers from postcards and claimed them as their own. (Courtesy Arizona Historical Society.)

MEXICAN WAR SERIES NO. 3

OUTSIDE OF CUSTOM HOUSE VERA CRUZ, AFTER SEIZURE OF SAME BY AMERICANS - APRIL 1914.

The invasion and occupation of Veracruz by United States military forces in April 1914 was the first event of the revolution that attracted the serious interest of large American manufacturers of printed postcards. The W. M. Prilay Post Card Company sent retail merchants one of its cards with a sales pitch printed on the message side: "This is a sample of the Mexican War Series. They come in 24 different designs and we supply agents at 50¢ per 100. We also enclose sample of Men and Lions Puzzle. How many of each shall we send you?" (Courtesy John Hardman Collection.)

Another major producer, the Max Stein Company of Chicago, issued this multiview with four scenes from Veracruz on a single postcard. (Courtesy John Hardman Collection.)

Cartoon postcards sold in steady, if unspectacular, quantities throughout
the postcard era. Given the wide interest throughout the United States in
the American occupation of Veracruz, it was predictable that the operation would result in its share of cartoonists' attempts at postcard humor.
(Courtesy John Hardman Collection.)

In Memoriam.
VERA CRUZ.

April 21, 1914.——ACROSTIC.——May 11, 1914.

Veiled to our sight, the hand of fate
Each one strikes down, now soon or late.
Remembered on the Roll of Fame
Are these young men, with honored name.

Called to the front for Country dear;
Reposed in death, our hearts their bier.
United stand, Land of the Free,
Zealous alway for Liberty.

Charles C. C. Cushing.   Brooklyn, New York

Like cartoon cards, postcards with poems—romantic, sentimental, or patriotic—were common. They could be made quickly and inexpensively, but the literary quality of the poetry was often very poor, not to speak of the spelling. (Courtesy Andreas Brown Collection.)

Mexican Naval cadets. The negative of this picture was found in camera in Naval Academy at Vera Cruz, Mexico, After being bombarded by Americans Apr. 22nd 14.

A Mexican naval cadet took this photo of his comrades. A member of the American invasion force found the cadet's camera, still loaded with exposed and unprocessed film, after the Naval Academy in Veracruz had been bombarded by the U.S. Navy and evacuated by the Mexicans. Whether the young photographer died during the shelling or merely fled, leaving his camera behind, is not known. (Courtesy Carter Rila Collection.)

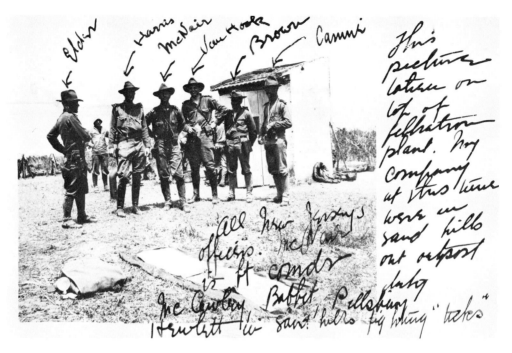

Darkrooms on American naval ships that participated in the attack on Veracruz contained equipment to produce photographic postcards for crew members. The presence of these officers on the grounds of a water filtration plant reflects the War Department's campaign to justify the Veracruz affair in terms of health and sanitation improvements brought by the invaders to the city. (Courtesy D. J. Sobery Collection.)

The landing batallion of the U.S.S. *New Jersey*, a total of 19 officers and 322 enlisted men, stayed ashore in Veracruz from April 22 to April 30, 1914. The ship's photographers recorded their embarkation on a U.S. Navy tugboat for transfer back to the *New Jersey*. (Courtesy D. J. Sobery Collection.)

VERA CRUZ,
MEXICO

CHRISTMAS,
1914

U. S. S. MINNESOTA

Best Wishes for
A Merry Christmas
and
A Happy and Prosperous New Year

American naval vessels remained on station at Veracruz for eight months. Crew members of the U.S.S. *Minnesota* sent this handsome Christmas postcard made aboard ship to family and friends back in the states. (Courtesy John Hardman Collection.)

The Ruins of Columbus, N.M. after being Raided by Pancho Villa.

W.H.Horne Co.
El Paso, Tex.

Villa's Columbus raid, the Punitive Expedition, and the American military buildup on the border created a huge national demand for postcards; enterprising manufacturers eagerly responded. When he learned of Villa's attack, Walter H. Horne of El Paso went immediately by automobile to Columbus and captured the still smoking ruins with his camera. He then hurried back to El Paso and got his postcards on the market before those of his competitors. This card became an especially big seller all across America. (Courtesy Carter Rila Collection.)

Reporters and photographers from major American newspapers and wire services converged on Columbus to accompany the Punitive Expedition into Mexico. General John J. Pershing posed for photographers and talked to reporters before leading his men across the border on March 15, 1916, but what he had to say did not please the members of the press corps: their coverage of the military campaign would be severely restricted, at least temporarily, by tough War Department censorship. (Courtesy Carter Rila Collection.)

Our Boys on the March in Mexico.

Copyrighted, Underwood & Underwood, N. Y.

When the censorship finally eased, the news stories and photographs that came out of Mexico tended to be rather dull. There was not much military action to report, and Pershing's forces never quite managed to track down Villa. Instead of combat scenes, countless postcards showed columns of soldiers and the truck convoys that supplied them traversing the desert and mountain terrain of northern Mexico. That was hardly what the "war correspondents" and "combat photographers" had in mind when they flocked to the border to chronicle the activities of the American troops in Mexico. (Both courtesy John Hardman Collection.)

931 A TRUCK TRAIN CROSSING CHOCOLATE PASS BETWEEN COLONIA
DUBLAN AND GALIANA IN MEXICO.
COPYRIGHTED BY INTERNATIONAL FILM SERVICE.

Troops of the Punitive Expedition fought a pitched battle against Carrancistas at Carrizal, Chihuahua, eighty miles south of Ciudad Juárez, on June 20, 1916. Forty-five Mexicans and fourteen Americans, including the two opposing commanding officers, died in a fierce fire fight. In addition, twenty-five Americans were taken prisoner. Among them were these black members of the Tenth Cavalry Regiment. The Carrizal incident brought Mexico and the United States to the brink of war, but negotiations resulted in a lessening of tension and the repatriation of the American prisoners. Walter H. Horne produced this famous postcard from a photograph or postcard made originally by a Mexican photographer. He did so in such haste that he did not even bother to obliterate the caption printed in Spanish. (Courtesy John Hardman Collection.)

The crisis resulting from the Carrizal incident made Americans more curious about Venustiano Carranza, so the Max Stein Company of Chicago reissued this postcard originally marketed in 1914. The caption incorrectly referred to him as a general. A civilian, Carranza took the title of First Chief of the Constitutionalist Forces. (Courtesy John Hardman Collection.)

GEN. PANCHO VILLA

U.S. Funeral

GEN. PANCHO VILLA RAID ON COLUMBUS, NEW MEXICO,
MARCH 9TH, AT 4 A. M., 1916. ALSO U. S. SOLDIERS KILLED IN
THE RAID. THE BODIES ARE READY FOR SHIPMENT HOME.
VILLA KILLED MEN AND WOMEN AND BURNED THE TOWN. U.
S. SOLDIERS ROUTED HIM, KILLING 200 OF HIS BANDITS, BURN-
ING THEIR BODIES.
NO. ___ 115   CAL. OSBON, PHOTOGRAPHER.
                                              DOUGLAS, ARIZONA.

Gen. Francisco Villa
the cause of it all   KAVANAUGH'S
                                          WAR
                                          POSTALS

Even though the failed military campaign in northern Mexico frustrated many Americans, it hardly diminished their interest in "Gen. Francisco Villa the cause of it all." Postcard manufacturers touched up pictures that they already had of Villa and made new postcards to capitalize on public demand. (Both courtesy John Hardman Collection.)

This multiview combines a picture of Villa with shots of Columbus and the Punitive Expedition. (Courtesy Carter Rila Collection.)

The general mobilization of the National Guard for service on the Mexican border proved to be a bonanza for postcard producers; the 184,000 guardsmen purchased huge quantities of postcards as souvenirs of their service and to send home. While postcards of scenes of guard units once on the border abound in collections, cards showing the men as they prepared to leave their respective states are quite rare. (Courtesy D. J. Sobery Collection.)

Members of the Third Oregon Infantry, stationed at Camp Tecate, California, pose for the camera on the border with their rifles at the ready, as if they expected an attack by Mexicans; at least that is what they wanted folks at home to believe. (Courtesy D. J. Sobery Collection.)

Before sending this card home, a militiaman used arrows to identify other members of his squad. (Courtesy John Hardman Collection.)

The guardsmen were particularly fond of postcards with pictures of themselves and their buddies. (Courtesy Carter Rila Collection.)

A postcard photographer would often get members of the same company to pose for an informal group portrait and then return a couple of days later to sell postcards to each of the men in the picture. (Courtesy Carter Rila Collection.)

As border duty wore on, soldier boys and photographers created more imaginative poses, which resulted in the production and sale of even more postcards. (Courtesy Carter Rila Collection.)

Some of the troops were willing to pay a little extra to be photographed in the basket of an observation balloon that appeared to be "high above camp."
(Courtesy John Hardman Collection.)

Of course, the guardsmen desired to send holiday greetings, so opportunistic entrepreneurs printed special postcards for men from units like the Thirteenth Pennsylvania Infantry. (Courtesy John Hardman Collection.)

Soliders from Grand Rapids, Michigan, sent this sentimental Thanksgiving postcard to loved ones in November
1916. (Courtesy Andreas Brown Collection.)

Venomous snakes of the Southwest must have seemed particularly exotic and dangerous to post-card recipients from other regions. (Courtesy El Paso Public Library.)

These two individuals, labelled "Typical Mexican Soldiers," conformed to (and even helped to strengthen) the stereotypical American image of Mexicans as a violent people. (Courtesy John Hardman Collection.)

Crap Game

The soldiers sent certain postcards, not to their mothers, but rather to old high school pals to let them see for themselves the excitement they were missing because they were not in the state militia. (Courtesy John Hardman Collection.)

Roulette at Monte Carlo, Juarez, Mex.

Nothing back home could match the drama of the roulette table at the infamous Monte Carlo Club, which had the dubious distinction of being singled out for especially negative commentary in a 1915 *Boston Herald* article on Ciudad Juárez entitled "The Most Wickedest City." (Courtesy El Paso Public Library.)

Another postcard to send to a friend, but certainly not to Mom, suggested that Mexican women had loose moral standards. (Courtesy Ralph Downey Collection.)

A SOLDIER STANDING IN THE U.S.
WITH HIS "ASS" IN MEXICO.

Troops with a rather crass sense of humor liked this postcard. A competing manufacturer made a nearly identical card. Both versions sold well. (Courtesy John Hardman Collection.)

While some guardsmen sent postcards that conveyed the impression that their service on the border was exciting, Jody P. Harris of the Texas National Guard did otherwise. The cartoons that he drew on penny postals and mailed to the Mineral Wells, Texas, drugstore, ridiculed the mobilization of his unit for duty in the Big Bend country because there were no Mexican invaders to fight. (Courtesy Sul Ross State University, Library Special Collections.)

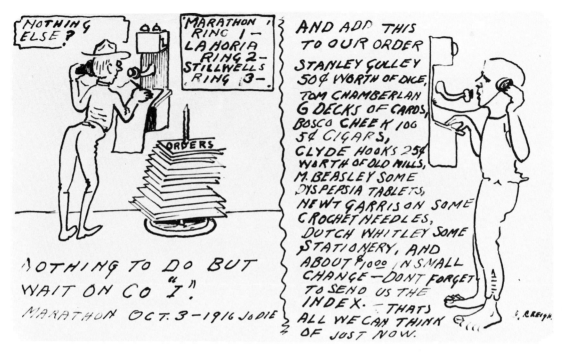

As the days and months passed, Harris became increasingly bored and resentful, but his cartoons prove that he never lost his caustic sense of humor. (Courtesy Sul Ross State University, Library Special Collections.)

One of the Many Y.M.C.A. Buildings Along the Border

Because of their popularity, postcards were widely available in cities and towns near military camps and in post exchanges and YMCAs on bases. The YMCAs were specifically intended to provide the men with wholesome Christian alternatives to the sleazy attractions of camp and border towns. (Courtesy Carter Rila Collection.)

These YMCA trucks, loaded with magazines, newspapers, postcards, and stationery, prepare to leave Deming, New Mexico, to resupply the YMCA branch at Colonia Dublán, Mexico, for the last time in January 1917. (Courtesy John Hardman Collection.)

Street Scene, Juarez, Mex.

Despite the existence of YMCAs, Mexican border towns, particularly Ciudad Juárez, had other diversions that the troops enjoyed. Yes, they bought postcards and "typical" Mexican souvenirs to send home. But Juárez also meant gambling and prostitution. One American writer labeled it "a typical Mexican frontier town of squat, one-story adobe houses . . . , of tiendas, plazas, casinos, bull rings, Chinese restaurants, curio stores, and often a few lurking American derelicts waiting here till the sheriffs of their home towns are dead." Another contemporary observer concluded that "Juárez harbors a few bad men of renown, but it entertains a swarm of swindlers, forgers, and crooks of low estate." (Courtesy John Hardman Collection.)

Almost as soon as Red Flag rebels captured Tijuana in May 1911 and raised their *Tierra y Libertad* (land and liberty) banner above the local post office, curious Americans streamed across the boundary from San Diego to take a close look at the *insurrecto* troops standing in the street and to buy "postal cards & curios." (Courtesy San Diego Historical Society—Ticor Collection.)

Vuendo el Combate desde El Paso.

Although thousands of "Mexican War post cards" made between 1911 and 1916 survive today, few depict postcard photographers at work. A Mexican photographer is responsible for this card that shows one of his American colleagues in El Paso pointing his camera at the combat going on just across the Rio Grande during the first battle of Ciudad Juárez in May 1911. (Courtesy Carter Rila Collection.)

A photographer using a Kodak 3A camera to take a picture of a Carrancista artillery battery preparing to fire on Villista troops in November 1915 during the second battle of Agua Prieta. (Courtesy Andreas Brown Collection.)

Spanish Soldiers shooting Cuban Spies.
Scene during the Revolution of 1895.

Mexican Federal Soldiers Shooting Spies

Villa's Firing Squad

Producers often reissued old postcards with new captions in response to changed market conditions. Some also shamelessly turned out cards with faked or posed scenes. The three postcards on these two pages published by H. H. Stratton of Chattanooga, Tennessee, provide classic examples of both practices. (All courtesy John Hardman Collection.)

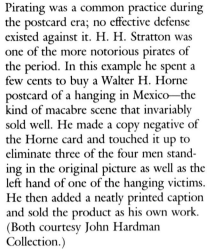

Pirating was a common practice during the postcard era; no effective defense existed against it. H. H. Stratton was one of the more notorious pirates of the period. In this example he spent a few cents to buy a Walter H. Horne postcard of a hanging in Mexico—the kind of macabre scene that invariably sold well. He made a copy negative of the Horne card and touched it up to eliminate three of the four men standing in the original picture as well as the left hand of one of the hanging victims. He then added a neatly printed caption and sold the product as his own work. (Both courtesy John Hardman Collection.)

Familiar Sceene in Mexico during the Revolution of the Past Three Years.

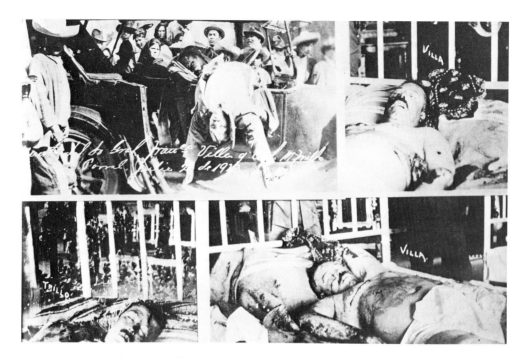

The assassination of Pancho Villa at Parral, Durango, on the morning of July 20, 1923 was a violent footnote to the Mexican Revolution that temporarily rekindled flagging postcard sales. The avalanche of gunfire that his personal and political enemies poured into Villa's Dodge instantly killed him and his secretary, Miguel Trillo. This multiview, made from pictures taken by local Mexican photographers, was one of several postcards produced by American manufacturers seeking to profit from public interest in the death of the colorful and controversial revolutionary chieftain. Such postcards were the last ones related to the Mexican Revolution to sell in significant numbers in the United States. (Courtesy Andreas Brown Collection.)

Chapter Two

A Small Entrepreneur Takes Advantage

Of all the photographers who made and sold real photo postcards capturing the Mexican Revolution and American military activity along the border, Walter H. Horne was by far the most successful. He arrived in El Paso in 1910 hiding in a railroad boxcar like a hobo because he was virtually penniless. By the time of his death in 1921, he had amassed a substantial estate. During his twelve-year residence in El Paso, Horne made money in activities ranging from hustling pool to operating shooting galleries, but he owed his remarkable rags-to-riches story primarily to extraordinary achievements in the postcard business. Horne's correspondence with members of his family in Maine documents his fascinating career; equally important, his cards and letters shed light on the nature of the photographic view card business during the postcard era in the United States.[1]

Walter Horne was born in Hallowell, Maine, in 1883, the youngest of several children of Henry and Susan Horne. In addition to the family farm, his father owned and operated a tanning business, which specialized in converting sheep skins into leather for shoes and harnesses.[2] While his older brother, Edward, remained in Hallowell to work with his father, Walter grew impatient with the limited opportunities that a small town in Maine offered to an ambitious young man. He went to New York City and by early 1905 had found employment with a firm in the financial district. He wrote to Edward on February 4 of that year and spoke of two critical factors that would shape his future: his contraction of tuberculosis and his determination to get rich. The first led him to El Paso, and the second partially explains his success in the postcard business there. He complained of a cold, a euphemism he continued to use when discussing his serious illness with family members. A bad cold had caused him "lots of trouble and lots of worry." Still, he boasted to his brother that he had recently handled bond transactions worth more than $4 million. Then referring to the opportunity to earn a large income in New York City, he said, "It's the only place."[3]

Despite Horne's desire to remain in New York, delicate health persuaded him to go west. In the period before antibiotics, tuberculosis was a dread disease, frequently resulting in chronic ill health and early death.[4] Most physicians advised consumptives, as victims of tuberculosis were called, to move to a warm, dry climate. It was thought that they would feel better and live longer in such an environment. After residing for a time in Denver, Colorado, Horne rode the freight trains to Los Angeles, California, in the fall of 1909. However, he did not particularly like southern California and, after briefly considering Arizona, decided to try El Paso.[5] Horne's trip to Texas was eventful. Once again he traveled in boxcars, and he later recounted to Edward that he was "pinched" by detectives four times en route but held in jail over night only once.[6] In February of 1910 Horne arrived in El Paso. Financially destitute, he gratefully accepted the $15 sent in the mail by his parents and brother.[7]

El Paso had a population of nearly forty thousand in 1910. The commercial, mining, and agricultural center of far west Texas, it was also the site of Fort Bliss, an army post with a garrison of two thousand men. Because of its dry climate the city enjoyed a reputation as an ideal residence for con-

sumptives, and the climate was certainly the major attraction to Horne.[8] El Paso's location on the Mexican border across the Rio Grande from Ciudad Juárez, Chihuahua, apparently had no influence on his decision to try his luck there. It simply turned out to be his unanticipated good fortune, and he took maximum advantage. Initially, however, Horne needed survival money. During his first year in El Paso, he worked at odd jobs and supplemented his wages with winnings from an occasional game of pool. At the same time, he continued to receive money fairly regularly from his family in Maine.[9]

By February 1911 Horne and increasing numbers of his fellow El Pasoans began to take an interest in the skirmishes between Mexican federal troops and insurgents near Ciudad Juárez.[10] While most of those who crossed the border to view the fighting regarded the activity merely as a diversion, Horne shrewdly saw the connection between the military conflict and the possibility of a profitable picture postcard business.[11] With no apparent previous interest in photography, he bought an inexpensive camera and the equipment necessary to turn out photographic postcards. Like many others throughout the United States during that era, he launched his postcard business with a very small initial investment. Unlike the overwhelming majority of others in the same line of work, however, Horne possessed exceptional entrepreneurial instincts and understood the consumer mentality. These qualities and the growing national market for cards depicting the Mexican Revolution and the American military response to it accounted for the success of his new venture.

By the time of the ferocious battle of Ciudad Juárez in May 1911, Horne already was making and selling postcards. On May 8, he mailed one with a picture of rebel leader Francisco Madero and members of his staff to his mother and told her: "I took this picture over at Madero's camp. There has been a lot of excitement down this way. All OK."[12] Two weeks later he wrote his sister, Gertrude, that he was busy taking pictures and making postcards.[13]

Despite this encouraging beginning, Horne still could not earn a living selling postcards. Once the battle of Ciudad Juárez ended and relative tranquility returned to the border region, sales of his postcards declined sharply; he urgently needed an additional source of income and set out to find one.[14] Horne and a partner left El Paso in June for New Mexico and Colorado to show moving pictures in towns and small cities that lacked theaters presenting films regularly. Horne took along a supply of his postcards with scenes of the revolution and managed to sell a good many of them. He also brought his camera and took pictures for those who wanted a postcard of themselves, their family members, or a local landmark.[15]

Horne enjoyed traveling about to show moving pictures and take photographs, but he earned little money. By September 9 he was back in El Paso, once again facing an uncertain future. His partner, who owned the movie projection equipment, was not anxious to go back on the road, and the continuing calm in Juárez and all along the international line augured poorly for the postcard business. A worried Horne wrote his mother, "There is talk . . . of another revolution. Hope it comes."[16] Two weeks

later he elaborated his concern: "The pictures of the Mexican Revolution don't amount to anything now. Am in hopes there will be more trouble across the river, but it is quiet there now."[17]

Not only was more trouble across the river slow to develop, but Horne's partner sold his moving picture outfit in early October to go into the saloon business.[18] At a time when he appeared to have very few money-making prospects, the resourceful Horne found a new use for his photographic equipment. He went to nearby Fort Bliss in October 1911 to take pictures of recently arrived members of the Fourth Cavalry.[19] These were the first; Horne eventually took thousands of photographs of troops along the border who wanted picture postcards of themselves to send to loved ones and friends back home. But the small garrison at Fort Bliss still produced relatively few sales, and between fall 1911 and late summer of the following year, Horne's earnings from his fledgling business were meager. His Christmas greetings to his family in 1911 acknowledged receipt of five dollars from Edward and added, "Wish I could send you all a good present for Christmas, but as it is—well—maybe next time."[20]

By spring, however, he was more optimistic:

Have been busy all week taking pictures around Ft. Bliss and the soldiers' camps along the river. Am in hopes to see the militia from some of the northern states come down here. If matters in Mexico get worse, the U.S. soldiers will very likely go across and that's what I want to see.[21]

While no American military expedition into Mexico

loomed, continuing revolutionary violence near the border produced a significant precautionary increase in troop strength at Fort Bliss and at small posts along the Rio Grande. The number of regular army soldiers stationed in El Paso and vicinity nearly doubled from about two thousand in February 1911 to almost four thousand in September 1912.[22] For the first time Horne began to make a decent profit from his business on a sustained basis. He wrote to his parents on September 30 that he had been busy for about a month taking pictures of soldiers and was doing "OK" financially.[23] He periodically sent similar financial reports to family members over the next thirteen months.[24]

The outbreak of the second battle of Ciudad Juárez in mid-November 1913 was an opportunity that Horne eagerly seized. He wrote his sister Gertrude triumphantly on November 24, "Got the best photos that ever came out of Mexico at the last battle of Juárez."[25] A month later he told her that postcard sales had been good.[26] By the third week of January 1914, he was even more optimistic and characterized business as "tip top." He had made over thirty thousand postcards, some of which he had sent in lots of one and two thousand to wholesalers in Atlantic City, New Jersey, and Los Angeles, California. He chided Gertrude for returning twenty-five dollars that he recently had sent to her. Appreciative of her loans to him when he was "down and out," he was finally getting on his feet financially and wanted her to keep any money that he sent to her.[27]

Walter Horne's monetary worries were over. After struggling to survive in the postcard business for over two and one-half years, he at last had established himself on a sound financial foundation. By early 1914 the second battle of Ciudad Juárez and an influx of refugees from northern Mexico into the El Paso area gave him the opportunity to take a number of pictures with good sales potential in postcard format and enabled him to augment substantially the income he already was earning by making view cards for the soldiers at Fort Bliss.

By April 1914 Horne was doing well enough to spend the substantial sum of one hundred and thirty-five dollars for a new Graflex camera to supplement his far-less-sophisticated equipment, probably a Kodak 3A.[28] The Eastman Kodak Graflex, widely regarded as the best professional camera made, was a single-lens reflex and had a focal plane shutter with a top speed of one one-thousandth of a second to photograph scenes with rapid motion. The Graflex also used cut film, which, unlike rolled film, could conveniently be exposed in single frames and immediately processed, an important advantage to a professional like Horne.[29] Horne took thousands of pictures of soldiers in the El Paso area with his new camera and turned them into postcards.

Meanwhile, national interest in events in Mexico increased greatly following the American military occupation of Veracruz in April 1914 and provided Horne with an expanded market for views in his inventory. By May of that year, he had shipped 7,800 postcards to New York City and had outstanding orders to fill for 16,000 more. He wrote his parents elatedly that he wanted them to enjoy a summer vacation at his expense. If they would tell him where they wished to go, he would send them the money, and he urged them to "make plans for a good trip."[30]

Horne's postcard business prospered throughout the remainder of 1914 and all of 1915. He faithfully photographed the troops stationed at local camps, and they bought increasing numbers of his postcards. At the same time he supplied wholesalers throughout the country with all the postcards they would handle.[31] Always eager for new sales, he journeyed to east Texas during the summer of 1914 and persuaded retail merchants in Galveston and Texas City to stock his postcards. He was particularly pleased to have his view cards placed on sale in post exchanges in the large army camp in Texas City.[32]

In December 1915 Horne invested some of his profits in a new business venture, a shooting gallery in El Paso to entertain soldiers during their off-duty hours.[33] In this activity, he formed a partnership with an individual named Henry E. Cottman that endured until the end of Horne's life in 1921. Although few details have surfaced about their business relationship, Horne probably remained responsible for the photography business, while Cottman managed the shooting gallery. The photographic component of the new partnership, the Mexican War Photo Postcard Company, had its own impressive letterhead stationery. Advertised products included photo postcards and enlarged views of the Mexican Revolution, typical Mexican scenes, bull fights, U.S. Army events, and Indian and other picturesque photographs of the Southwest. All could be purchased on a wholesale or retail basis.[34]

No one benefited as much from the sharp increase in demand for Mexican Revolution postcards in 1916 as did Walter Horne, who had stockpiled a large inventory of negatives from shots that he had been taking in Mexico since 1911. When the

Figure 1. A Graflex camera manufactured in 1907. This and later models of the durable and dependable Graflex remained favorites of postcard and press photographers through the late 1920s. (Photograph by Frank N. Samponaro.)

bull market for postcards hit, he turned them out in ever larger quantities—printing a wide variety of views from his supply of negatives, even though some of the scenes were five years old. An uncritical public, anxious to get any look at the action along the border, did not know the difference and bought many more of his cards than ever before. Shots that he took as early as the first battle of Juárez in May 1911 were once again in demand, but his best-selling single group of cards pictured the execution of three Mexicans in Ciudad Juárez in January 1916; it became known as the "triple execution" series.

Horne's triple execution postcard coup called into action his extraordinary entrepreneurial skills. When he learned that General Gabriel Gavira, the Carrancista commandant of the federal army garrison in Ciudad Juárez, had ordered the execution of three men for allegedly stealing military supplies, Horne immediately recognized the unusual opportunity for profit that the gruesome event offered him. He knew that spectacular macabre scenes sold postcards, and over the past five years, he had made the personal acquaintance of authorities involved in the drama unfolding across the border. Using his contacts in Juárez, Horne got in touch with the officer in charge of the firing squad, Captain Javier J. Valle, and paid him a "mordida" (bribe) for exclusive rights to photograph the executions. At 11:30 on the morning of January 15, the three condemned prisoners were marched between rows of soldiers to the south wall of the Northwest Railroad Station. Horne, in position with his Graflex on a tripod, nodded to Captain Valle that he was ready. The Mexican officer then ordered his men to take

aim and fire. The first victim, Francisco Rojas, fell straight backward as puffs of dust rose from the adobe wall where the bullets struck. Within minutes the same ghastly procedure had been repeated twice, and Juan Aguilar and José Moreno also lay dead in the dirt. Following the final volley of shots, Horne's employees worked the large crowd. Curious onlookers who had crossed the river from El Paso to witness the well-publicized executions could order photographic souvenirs of the event. For twenty-five cents, the photographer guaranteed mail delivery, within ten days, of three view cards of the executions. Although Horne received numerous orders that day for his triple execution postcards, the total was insignificant compared to the number he sold when he reissued them during the military buildup on the border in the summer of 1916. From commanding generals to privates, they all bought the cards; most of the collections reviewed for this book contain the famous series.[35]

Villa's Columbus raid on March 9 and the subsequent concentration of more than 180,000 troops along the border gave Horne the chance to make the kind of money that he had dreamed of earning ever since his days in the financial district in New York City; he was determined to make the most of it. On March 15 Horne returned from Columbus with a "scoop."[36] Referring to himself and an unnamed employee, he bragged:

We were the first ones into Columbus with cameras, and the first ones out with negatives, consequently we beat them all to the newspapers; got our stuff into Chicago, New York, Boston, Atlanta, San Francisco over twelve hours ahead of the others, and believe we will make some money out of it. These papers are dead anxious for photos, and we have been swamped with telegrams for new stuff. . . . We are getting out postcards as fast as possible; have two men and two girls working so I believe we are in the way of making some money.

The censor is strict, but this is to our advantage as we have been photographing for years, and have many negatives from which we are printing and which other photographers which have just arrived will not be able to get.[37]

Not content with his Columbus bonanza and the prospect of dramatically increased sales of postcard reissues, Horne soon found another source of profit. The War Department imposed strict, if only temporary, censorship on the news reporters and photographers who hurried to the border to follow Pershing's forces into Mexico. When the Punitive Expedition crossed the international boundary south of Columbus on March 15, the censorship rules prohibited accompanying news photographers from taking any pictures.[38] These regulations did not impede Walter Horne; in fact, they allowed him to get exclusive pictures of the expedition. Horne shrewdly made an agreement in Columbus with an experienced army photographer, Corporal C. Tucker Beckett of the Sixteenth Infantry, to take pictures for him when Beckett's unit went into Mexico as part of the invading force. The corporal had previously collaborated with Horne in a mutually profitable studio at Fort Bliss, which produced portrait photographs of soldiers of the Sixteenth Infantry. Now Beckett promised to take pictures in Mexico with his Kodak 3A camera and send the unprocessed rolls of film through the U.S. Army post to Horne in El Paso. In return, Horne agreed to pay

him for any exposures that he decided to use. Horne turned many of Beckett's shots into postcards; he also sold a number of them to newspapers thirsting for pictorial material from the border and claimed the images as his own on the credit line.

The arrangement between Horne and Beckett, however, was of relatively brief duration. By the early summer of 1916, the War Department considerably relaxed censorship restrictions on the legion of photographers who had accompanied the Punitive Expedition into Mexico. Large numbers of picture postcards and newspaper photographs with scenes of what had become a rather dull military campaign soon appeared, and the supply quickly exceeded the demand. Realizing the changed market conditions, Horne abruptly terminated his agreement with Beckett and focused his attention on a new source of postcard profit.[39]

The general mobilization of the National Guard ordered by President Wilson on June 18 and the concentration of forty thousand troops in the El Paso region by mid-summer provided Horne with a major new clientele for postcards. The guardsmen bought huge quantities of Mexican Revolution postcards made by Horne and his competitors in stores and at newstands in downtown El Paso and at post exchanges and YMCAs on military bases. Tracy Hammond Lewis, a correspondent for the *New York Morning Telegraph,* who was in El Paso during July and August 1916, wrote that while many scenes of the revolution were popular, the first postcard in Horne's triple execution series was the soldiers' "favorite."[40] In addition to doing a very profitable trade reprinting views in his inventory for the guardsmen in the El Paso area, Horne also aggressively sold reissues to dealers in towns throughout the Southwest where other military camps were located.[41]

Despite the very good money he was already making, Horne saw the massive concentration of troops in the vicinity of El Paso as an unparalleled opportunity for further sales. He began to photograph the growing horde of guardsmen in a methodical, systematic manner. As Horne anticipated, they posed eagerly and bought his postcards with pictures of themselves and their buddies to send back home. While many of Horne's postcards of the militiamen were unimaginative, rather tedious, and posed, they sold in great quantities. In July Horne, whose exclusive concern was of course profits, not aesthetics, wrote his mother enthusiastically that great times had arrived.[42] A week and a half later he exulted:

Business is simply great, and as my opportunity has arrived, am making every effort to get the benefit from my negatives, which have cost me a good deal of hard work and trouble.

Am making *5,000 postcards* a day. Supply post exchanges + stores all along the border. . . . Shall go to Deming, N. Mex tomorrow to shoot up the Delaware troops. Big camp there.[43]

Great financial times had indeed arrived for Walter Horne, but ambition spurred him on. By the summer of 1916, he and Cottman owned two more shooting galleries, one in El Paso and the other in Columbus.[44] Like the first one, the two newer galleries were in business to relieve the off-duty soldiers of their pocket money and soon were operating quite profitably. The cost of equipping a

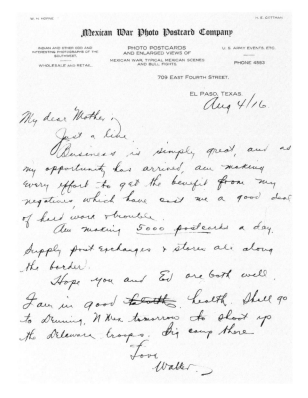

Figure 2. Walter Horne's letter of August 4, 1916 to his mother. (Courtesy El Paso Public Library.)

single shooting gallery approached fifteen hundred dollars, but thanks to his income from soaring postcard sales, Horne had no difficulty coming up with his share of the investment for the new galleries.[45]

No precise information exists on how long Horne continued to make five thousand postcards a day or whether he ever exceeded that rate of pro-duction. Nevertheless, the large numbers of his cards that survive in collections of varying sizes throughout the United States verify that he outsold any of his competitors by a wide margin during the peak sales period of the spring and summer of 1916. Horne's rivals included small operators like Frank C. Hecox of El Paso, medium-size firms like Kavanaugh's War Postals of Chicago and El Paso, and large concerns like the Max Stein Company of Chicago and the International Film Service of New York. The market was so big in 1916 that most of those who made Mexican Revolution postcards shared in the prosperity. Nevertheless, the custom-ary unscrupulousness of some postcard producers continued. At least two manufacturers of printed postcards, the Max Stein Company of Chicago and H. H. Stratton of Chattanooga, pirated several of Horne's views and sold them as their own. Horne probably did not worry very much about this unau-thorized use of his images. A certain amount of pir-ating was an occupational hazard, and he may have done some of his own. While postcard pirating was merely an irritation, an increasingly popular new medium seemed capable of having an adverse impact on Horne's booming postcard sales.

By 1916 most cities in the United States, including El Paso, had more than one theater that showed a newsreel per week, usually as a prelude to feature films.[46] One American newsreel made in 1911 contains brief scenes of the destruction caused by the first battle of Ciudad Juárez.[47] But significant attention on the part of American filmmakers to the Mexican Revolution dates from 1914, when Pancho Villa concluded a remarkable arrangement with the Mutual Film Corporation of New York City. Mutual guaranteed Villa twenty-five thousand dol-lars in return for the exclusive right to accompany him in the field and photograph his battles. Other revolutionary chieftains, including Alvaro Obregón, soon signed similar contracts with other motion pic-ture companies.[48]

U.S. public interest in Mexican affairs swelled at the time of the American military landing in Veracruz in April 1914, and newsreel film compa-nies dispatched crews to the Mexican port city to photograph the occupation.[49] One of them, the Sawyer Film Mart of New York City, promised "the actual scenes of the fighting, the dead and wounded as they dropped in battle, our boys working with machine guns with deadly effect."[50] While such foot-age proved popular, the combat in Veracruz involv-ing Americans lasted only a short time. After it stopped, newsreels shown in American theaters con-tained only occasional glimpses of the Mexican Rev-olution, which no longer could compete for public attention with scenes of the bloody fighting in Europe.[51] Then, Villa's attack on Columbus and the beginning of the Punitive Expedition made Mexico good box office once again. One advertisement melo-dramatically urged, "SEE your flag across the border to punish those who have insulted it."[52] Another promised "absolutely authentic startling realism, thrilling fights, 2,000 feet of sensations direct from Mexico."[53]

These financially successful films had a negligi-ble impact on postcard sales, however. Within a week of Villa's attack on Columbus on March 9, 1916, Horne had marketed thousands of cards showing the damage and destruction, while the first

Figure 3.   Although not yet a threat to photographic postcard sales, newsreels had become popular by 1916. Numerous small distributors competed intensely for the business of movie theaters, as evidenced in these advertisements from April 1916 issues of *Moving Picture World.*

motion pictures with scenes from Columbus were not available for national distribution until the beginning of April.[54] Since most newsreel film companies had their headquarters in the eastern United States, the unexposed film had to be sent there to be processed and copied before being distributed to theaters across the country.[55] Because of this slow, cumbersome procedure, a producer of photo postcards like Horne enjoyed the important advantage of timeliness over the newsreel industry. Furthermore, millions of Americans living in rural areas rarely, if ever, saw moving pictures and continued to rely on postcards for visual images of the attack on Columbus, the Punitive Expedition, and other news events.

While Horne overcame the pirating of competitors and the proliferation of newsreels, the withdrawal of Pershing's troops from Mexico, the recall of National Guard units from the border, and growing national preoccupation with the war in Europe devastated the postcard business. A brief sojourn in 1917 to Deming, New Mexico, to photograph World War I recruits proved profitable but did not reverse the trend. Surviving correspondence from Horne to members of his family in Maine is scanty after December 1917 and ceases completely in July 1919, when Horne was in failing health and no longer selling as many postcards. The money that he was earning now appeared to come principally from the shooting galleries that he and his partner continued to run.[56] By this time, however, Horne had attained the kind of financial security achieved by few other photographic postcards makers. He wrote to his mother in August 1917:

. . . we are strictly in the money out here, and in pretty fair health at present, and I can quit business any time and never have to worry about money matters. I have had a lot of trouble since I came out here with poor health, otherwise would have been rich by this time.[57]

Horne fell gravely ill in the fall of 1921. His brother Edward, summoned to El Paso, wrote his fiancee in Maine, "Walter has got a lot of money, much more than I ever dreamed he had."[58] Walter Horne finally succumbed to tuberculosis on October 13, 1921 at the age of thirty-eight.[59] In his will he left one thousand dollars to Adelina Zuvia Horne, the woman he married on July 21, 1921. He also established a trust fund of three thousand dollars for their infant son, Edward Elmer Horne, and designated his brother as the trustee. Practically nothing is known of Adelina Zuvia Horne; Horne apparently met her late in his short life. Nearing death, he fulfilled his personal responsibilities, married Adelina Zuvia, and provided for her and their son in his will. The remainder of his estate, an unknown amount, went to his mother. Among the witnesses who signed Horne's will was his partner, Henry E. Cottman.[60]

Horne's comfortable status at the time of his death derived primarily from his extraordinary success in the postcard business. He started out on a shoestring but at the right time and place. To this fortunate circumstance Horne applied a relentless determination to make money and truly exceptional entrepreneurial talents. His motivation in turning out literally hundreds of thousands of postcards was exclusively financial. There is no suggestion in his correspondence that he had the slightest interest in the Mexican Revolution or its international political ramifications, except as they related to his business. He did not intend to record history, yet he did so. Thousands of his postcards form the core of virtually all the remarkably rich private and public collections that are the indispensable basis for this book.

Pascual Orozco
1140.

PASCUAL
OROZCO
EN C JUAREZ

From the outset of his career as a postcard photographer, Walter H. Horne demonstrated an ability to get good-quality close-up pictures of the leaders of the revolution. One of his earliest was of the rebel field general Pascual Orozco and an aide immediately following the first battle of Ciudad Juárez in May 1911. Events later forced Orozco into exile, and when he tried to mount an offensive from Texas in 1915, he was tracked down and killed like a common cattle rustler. Horne took advantage of the spectacular incident to reissue this postcard. (Courtesy El Paso Public Library.)

Felix Diaz.
Associated with Pres. Huerta
at
Mexico City.

Horne did not often make postcards from portrait photographs, but he correctly calculated that the notoriety surrounding Felix Díaz, nephew of the ousted Mexican ruler,
who was implicated in the conspiracy against Francisco
Madero, would create public demand for this picture.
(Courtesy El Paso Public Library.)

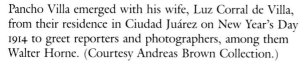

Pancho Villa emerged with his wife, Luz Corral de Villa, from their residence in Ciudad Juárez on New Year's Day 1914 to greet reporters and photographers, among them Walter Horne. (Courtesy Andreas Brown Collection.)

Horne made this portrait of an unusually dapper-looking Villa when the general visited El Paso to confer with American officials in January 1915. Horne reissued the popular card periodically over the next two years and did so with particular financial success following Villa's Columbus raid in March 1916. (Courtesy El Paso Public Library.)

Horne mailed this postcard to his father on April 2, 1914.
On the back he asked: "This is Gen. Carranza now located in
Juárez. What do you think of him?" (Courtesy El Paso Pub-
lic Library.)

Horne methodically documented with his camera the arrivals and departures of Mexican revolutionary leaders in El Paso and Ciudad Juárez. He took this photograph when General Alvaro Obregón and his staff visited the Mexican border city on May 4, 1916, including left to right: Major Alberto G. Montaño, Major Rafael T. Villagrán, Balomero A. Almada, Major J. M. Carpio, A. G. García, General Alvaro Obregón, Captain A. de Saracho, Captain A. Gaxiola, General F. R. Serrano, and Colonel Aarón Sáenz. Besides issuing his picture as a postcard, Horne also sold a copy of it to the *El Paso Herald,* which printed it on page one of its May 5 edition. During this period Horne regularly supplied the *Herald* with photographs, including shots of the Punitive Expedition in Mexico that he received from Corporal C. Tucker Beckett. (Courtesy El Paso Public Library.)

Horne visited the scene of the fighting following the second battle of Ciudad Juárez in November 1913. (Courtesy Nita Stewart Haley Memorial Library.)

Like others in his business Horne knew that scenes of death sold particularly well and sought to capitalize upon public fascination with the macabre. (Courtesy Carter Rila Collection.)

By January 1914 Horne did a brisk business supplying wholesalers on both east and west coasts with postcards in lots of one and two thousand. Although these customers invariably preferred cards with pictures of combat and death, those with "typical" Mexican scenes were also in demand. (Courtesy Carter Rila Collection.)

Horne sent postcards to his wholesale and retail customers with captions meant to enhance their sales potential. (Courtesy Carter Rila Collection.)

Horne's postcards consistently reinforced the negative American stereotype of "typical Mexicans," a view Horne himself shared. When he sent this card to his mother on September 3, 1912, he explained: "One of many groups of women who follow up the Mexican Army preparing dinner. Note the pool of filth. The fleas don't show." (Courtesy El Paso Public Library.)

Uncle Sam's Guests at Fort Bliss, Tex.

Still, Horne expressed compassion for refugees who had fled Mexico in December 1913, when Villa captured Ojinaga. He wrote his sister, Gertrude, a postcard postmarked January 23, 1914: "4987 Mexico refugees arrived in El Paso yesterday and today. Probably 1,000 of them women and children. The most pitiful sight I ever saw in my life. They are now in a government camp at Fort Bliss. This is only one of a number of photos I will send you. Took a *good* number today." (Courtesy El Paso Public Library.)

Horne went to Fort Bliss for the first time in October 1911 to photograph the soldiers. He returned a day or two later to sell the men postcards of themselves and their comrades. Cards such as this one, dated 1912, sold in small quantities, but production costs were so low that Horne still earned a penny on each card he sold. (Courtesy El Paso Public Library.)

Horne used his Graflex camera to "stop the action" during cavalry maneuvers at Fort Bliss in 1914. On the back of one of the postcards in this series, he wrote Gertrude: "Have put out a big bunch of these the past two weeks. How are those I sent a long time ago? Am curious to know if they turn yellow. Suppose they do, as I don't bother to wash them much." (Courtesy El Paso Public Library.)

In addition to making photocards to sell to troops at Fort Bliss and other area military camps, Horne regularly produced cards that appealed primarily to the civilian residents of El Paso. His subjects included local landmarks, like buildings and parks, and special events, like this Flag Day parade on June 14, 1916 in which both soldiers and local civilians marched. (Courtesy El Paso Public Library.)

Deadly Poisonous Gila Monster. Found on the Deserts of the Southwest.

W.H.Horne Co. El Paso Tex.

Troops from northern states wanted to impress folks at home with the ruggedness of military service on the border, so they sent them postcards of "dangerous" desert creatures like this gila monster. (Courtesy El Paso Public Library.)

This postcard of "American Insurrectos" in action is obviously posed, but it fooled a lot of people and sold in large numbers. (Courtesy Andreas Brown Collection.)

Whether the man seated on the step was really a rebel who had killed ten federal soldiers after being shot in the foot did not matter to Horne, whose caption made the postcard highly marketable. (Courtesy John Hardman Collection.)

Horne's work was frequently pirated by other photographers. Max Stein's multiview, "Scenes of the Mexican Revolution," is made up of three Horne originals, plus one, "Mexican Sharp-shooters," by an unknown publisher. (Courtesy Sam Stark Collection.)

Horne turned out this postcard of an army truck convoy in Columbus, New Mexico, in mid-1916. Within a few weeks a pirated version had been marketed by Dak Roogelo, Incorporated; Horne's name was removed and a new caption added: "Motor Train Camp Travis, San Antonio, Texas." (Courtesy Carter Rila Collection.)

The triple execution series was particularly profitable for Horne, and he reissued the three popular postcards repeatedly during 1916 to fulfill demand along newly arrived National Guard troops. Francisco Rojas was the first to die in front of the wall of the Northwest Railroad Station in Ciudad Juárez on the morning of January 15, 1916. Captain Javier J. Valle commanded the firing squad. Horne sent this card to Gertrude: "Took photos of three executions today. Here is the first one. The bullets have gone through the man. Notice the dust from the above wall back of him." (Courtesy El Paso Public Library.)

The execution of Juan Aguilar.
(Courtesy John Hardman Collection.)

The death of José Moreno. The postcards of their executions gave Rojas,
Aguilar, and Moreno far greater notoriety in death than they ever attained in
life. The *Historia gráfica de la revolución
Mexicana* later reproduced Horne's
image of the execution of Francisco
Rojas and described him as a Villista
labor organizer. (Courtesy John
Hardman Collection.)

In addition to photographing the three executions, Horne took other pictures in Ciudad Juárez on January 16 and turned them into postcards. Many of those who purchased the triple execution series bought these cards as well. The spectacle attracted a huge crowd (above) that gawked at the corpses (right above) and at the doctor's examination (right below). (above: Courtesy Carter Rila Collection, right above: Courtesy John Hardman Collection, right below: Courtesy Sam Stark Collection.)

Bodies of 3 men lying as they fell after being executed

Ruins of Commercial Hotel, Columbus, N.M) in which 6 Americans were killed and Their Bodies Cremated

W.H. Horne Co.
El Paso, Tex.
3018

Horne rushed back to El Paso with the film he took after Villa's Columbus raid and quickly distributed his images to newspapers and as postcards to an eager public. (Courtesy John Hardman Collection.)

The Bodies of Dead Bandits found all along the Trail of Pancho Villa.

Horne paused in the desert outside of Columbus for this picture which proved to Americans that at least one Villista had been made to pay for his crime. (Courtesy Carter Rila Collection.)

Motor Truck Train ready
to Enter Mexico.

W.H. Horne Co.
El Paso, Tex.

Horne returned to Columbus to photograph the concentration of troops and equipment under the command of General John J. Pershing. (Courtesy Carter Rila Collection.)

The caption on this postcard exemplifies the jingoistic public attitude that Horne exploited to maximize sales. (Courtesy Andreas Brown Collection.)

Horne did not accompany Pershing's forces into Mexico. Instead he hired a member of the expedition, Corporal C. Tucker Beckett, to send him images of the dramatic event. (Courtesy Carter Rila Collection.)

When he printed postcards from film he received from Beckett, Horne claimed credit in the captions for the photography in accordance with his agreement with the corporal. (Courtesy John Hardman Collection.)

This popular Horne postcard provided many Americans with their first look at the Punitive Expedition. (Courtesy El Paso Public Library.)

With Beckett supplying film from Mexico, Horne concentrated on photographing the buildup of National Guard forces in camps in the El Paso area. (Courtesy Carter Rila Collection.)

The national guardsmen never tired of buying cards of themselves and their friends. Horne obliged the boys and went to the camps day after day to take additional pictures and sell more postcards. (Both courtesy Carter Rila Collection.)

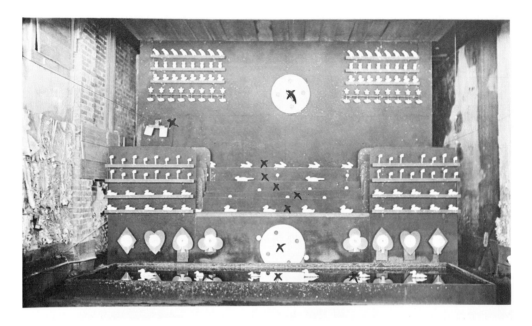

Horne earned enough money selling postcards to become part owner of shooting galleries in El Paso, Columbus, and Deming. He and Henry E. Cottman spent $1,437.12 to equip this one at 209 Broadway in El Paso. (Courtesy El Paso Public Library.)

• *Chapter Three* •

Border Fury

Mexico's 1910 Revolution sputtered to a start. Francisco I. Madero directed his followers to rebel on November 20, but few responded. There are no picture postcards of the event: no one thought the uprising would amount to much. Some Mexicans supported the Díaz dictatorship; others suspected that it could not be overturned and feared reprisals; many were too mired in their daily lives to give revolution much thought.

In the north, however, in the Valley of Papigochic, where the plains of the state of Chihuahua begin to build into the eastern slope of the Sierra Madre, the revolt took a tenuous hold among a handful of farmers, petty tradesmen, and minor administrators. The people of Papigochic had repeatedly asserted their freedom from the edicts and controls of Mexico City; they insisted they knew best what was good for them. The Papigochic Valley offered a variety of money-making opportu-

nities, and the residents understood the possibilities of profit and improvement. Ideals of liberty and justice articulated by Mexican exiles in the United States had permeated the locale and quickened its pulse, and, critically important, proximity to the U.S. border facilitated arms procurement and offered rebels refuge from the dictator's army. In overview for the region, a high level of political and economic consciousness abetted a minimal fear of government retaliation.[1]

Like a good many Mexicans, the people of Papigochic had their grievances—perceived, invented, and real—against the regime. The autocrat Porfirio Díaz and his benefactors and minions had manipulated power to suit themselves for three decades, more than a generation. Political discourse had become constricted at every level. Investment, much of it foreign, fueled growth, but the uncertainties of international economics caused development to lurch ahead in unsettling fits and starts, which benefited some and bankrupted others. The government often received the blame for the failures. With many Mexicans seeking to take advantage of the opportunities offered by the new order, competition for the proceeds was fierce at each social level, and those who prospered sought to expand their holdings and profits mindless of the cost to others. As a result, a good many Mexicans anxious for improvement were shunted to the perimeter of national development. Because the government and its judicial system normally defended the rich and the entrenched against those who sought a share in the new wealth, authorities at every level earned the animosity of the excluded. Pushed far enough, the malcontents resolved to force a change.

The vast majority of ordinary Mexicans only wanted to be left alone to continue the ways which had long served themselves and their ancestors, but development made no distinctions. The disruption drove some even further into debt and degradation; a few sensed the new national mood as a way to escape traditional fetters. For a variety of reasons, a good many Mexicans were astir, and some took the step from restlessness to revolution.

Although humanly degrading domestic conditions created discontent and even protest and spilled occasional blood, much of the conflict was confined to the local level, where the poor and the privileged met face to face. The contest was rarely fair, and protected partisans of the dictatorship normally won, which is not to say they were always legally wrong and morally unjust. By melding power and propaganda, brute force tempered by largesse, authoritarian pronouncements mellowed by com-

promise, Díaz and his supporters constructed a remarkable if unstable political edifice which earned international acclaim. Respect for Díaz the man and fear of his reprisals steadied the dictatorship, and the nation moved into the first decade of the twentieth century with no reason to expect that the chaos of revolution approached.

Then Díaz blundered. Either he did not understand that the power of a careless comment elevated to policy status can undo a state, or he was so self-assured that he thought he could be arrogant. In March 1908 he told an admiring American journalist that he believed his country was at last ready for democracy, and that in upcoming elections he would welcome competing political parties. Did Díaz mean it? Judging by his later actions, certainly not, but it was too late to retract what was already in print.

Mexicans took him at his word and did so with a long-repressed fervor. Candidates backed by an awakened electorate challenged Porfirian favorites for governorships in the states of Morelos and Sinaloa, and the wealthy Coahuila property owner Francisco Madero, intelligent, idealistic, stubborn, eccentric, announced his candidacy for the presidency in 1910. Díaz caught the scent of public sentiment and recanted, urged on by supporters who understood the danger to their interests. Mexico, on second thought, was not yet ready for democracy.

Official repression ensured victory for the dictator's choices in the 1909 state elections. Then, in the spring of 1910, Madero's energetic campaigning aroused unprecedented enthusiasm for his candidacy. Díaz had him arrested and jailed, pending the June elections. Once returned by ballot control to his seventh consecutive presidential term, the now eighty-year-old Díaz released Madero on bail. Madero promptly fled to San Antonio, Texas, where he issued his call to revolution, promising free elections and embracing the principle of no re-elections. The rebel leader wisely decided to stay in Texas when his promised Army of Liberation failed to materialize. The border protected him, while the people of Papigochic nourished his revolt.[2]

The border zone between the United States and Mexico has long served as a refuge for dissidents, as well as a lucrative, if often illegal, marketplace for entrepreneurs. The international boundary line itself has never more than slightly inconvenienced those who crossed it in either direction in search of betterment or relief. Residents of the zone, as well as others who understand its nature and potential, view the line more as opportunity than barrier.[3] Mexico's revolution greatly multiplied those opportunities.

The revolution gained momentum in early 1911 when the people of Papigochic proved that the troops of the dictator could be confronted and defeated. Their victories and standoffs encouraged rebel bands to sprout up in other regions of the republic. Díaz at first replied with bombast, assuring Mexicans and foreign interests of his will and ability to stamp out the brushfires. But when he opened secret (and quickly exposed) negotiations with his adversaries, the revolutionaries reasoned that dictators do not negotiate from strength, and they steadily upped the ante for peace. First they demanded a few changes in the cabinet, some governorships, then everything: Díaz must go.[4]

If Díaz capitulated, who would protect the more than $1 billion that Americans had invested in oil, railroads, timber, mining, agriculture, and other interests? U.S. President William Howard Taft was not sure. Taft had hoped that "the old man's official life will extend beyond mine. . . ." He had previously predicted that if Díaz died in office, turmoil over the succession question would require the U.S. to "interfere." Now revolution had come, and Taft had to face up to "a problem of the utmost difficulty."[5]

Taft temporized on the issue of neutrality; officially the U.S. would not permit the exportation of revolution from its soil against a friendly power. Taft prohibited the export of weapons and ammunition as well as manpower. Nonetheless, he had not moved aggressively to suffocate Madero's well-known plot, nor had his customs agents tried to blockade the shipment of war materiel meant for the rebels. Only in March 1911, when informed by his ambassador in Mexico that the Díaz dictatorship seemed near collapse, did Taft act. First, he announced enforcement of the neutrality laws: no weapons nor any war goods to the rebels. Then he called out the army—or at least a full two-thirds of the nation's mobile force (20,000 men)—to patrol the border. Publicly he termed the mobilization "seasonal maneuvers"; privately he was preparing for armed intervention, for war that is, if so ordered by Congress. Interventionists and noninterventionists in both public and private American life vigorously debated the possibilities and consequences of invasion, while Mexicans vowed to resist with force any intrusion on their national sovereignty.[6]

The U.S. Army was, at the time, third rate

(Japan had 700,000 soldiers and Germany more than one million) and widely dispersed. Forty-nine small detachments drilled in camps and outposts throughout the country or performed military duty in the Philippines and Caribbean. Few Americans saw a need for a large standing army; no one threatened U.S. territory. The army's only invasion plan (Plan Green) targeted Mexico. It took international shocks like the sinking of the Lusitania and Pancho Villa's raid on Columbus, New Mexico, to rally support for a modernized military, and even then the nation prepared sluggishly.[7]

The army may have somewhat professionalized, its ranks filled with career-minded volunteers, but in terms of mentality, style, preparedness, command, and training, the army was in major ways barely out of the Indian wars. It took the War Department six weeks just to round up enough men to send to the border: cavalry from Georgia; signal corps from Nebraska; infantry from Minnesota, Indiana, and Wyoming; engineers from Kansas.[8]

Once on the line, the army displayed its inability to carry out national policy. Its numbers were not nearly sufficient to patrol nearly 2,000 miles of rugged, often desolate, even hostile border. General Philip Sheridan tasted enough alkali dust from the region to conclude that if he owned both places, he would rent Texas and live in Hell; soldiers experiencing their first meetings with rattlesnakes and scorpions suggested that the U.S. go to war with Mexico and force it to take back the border zone. Furthermore, the resident Mexicans and Mexican-Americans were in nearly total sympathy with the revolution and determined to abet it. Evading

military patrols was no problem: they knew the territory.[9]

The military mandate was made no easier by private businessmen and public officials who determined to profit by channeling materiel to either rebel or federal troops—whoever paid up. Pragmatic folks, they sniffed opportunity in the instability of the revolution. Merchants, mercenaries, recruitment specialists, detectives, information grubbers, spies and counterspies, agents, double and triple agents all took advantage of the situation. Politicians raised a ruckus in their own behalf, and there were risks as well as profits. A fortunate German storekeeper in Presidio, Texas, who experienced a financial windfall with his shop and poolhall, had to keep his three daughters locked in the attic over the store and away from his more free-spirited customers.[10]

To make matters even worse for the U.S. soldiers, insurgents on the other side of the boundary began to threaten Mexican border towns in their search for a port of entry through which arms and ammunition could pour even more freely. In early May 1911, the prize sought was Ciudad Juárez, across the Rio Grande from El Paso. Juárez was well worth the fight. Its capture could bring down Díaz, or at least earn diplomatic recognition; the United States could declare the rebels belligerents and alter neutrality laws in their favor, facilitating the procurement of war goods.

Border warfare, however, created special international problems. In the firefights which engulfed these towns, some actually split by the international line, bullets inevitably sprayed U.S. territory, endangering American lives and property. American authorities then demanded the Mexicans contain their fight within their own territory or chance U.S. intervention. American citizens, who turned revolution watching into a spectator sport, greatly complicated the situation. An El Paso veteran of such spectacle remarked, "The majority of people here are now very familiar with the whine of high power guns in action," and they dodged—did a little mirthful twist—as a bullet whistled by. "Certainly you realized that when you heard the bullet, it had already passed, but as a matter of form you were entitled to a dodge."[11]

All of this romantic excitement, plus the sudden appearance of a new and certain market—soldier boys far from home and in some sort of action at last—spawned the region's hotly competitive and potentially lucrative picture postcard business. For the next six or seven years (until World War I absorbed much of the military market and almost all public interest), business boomed and waned in relation to the intensity of American military response to Mexico's revolution.

•

A certain card (reproduced with others at the end of the chapter) shows a postmark of June 3, 1911.[12] There they are, photographed a month earlier, hundreds and hundreds of El Paso people, perched high, two and three deep, on wooden railway cars, scanning south across the Rio Grande toward their sister border city, Ciudad Juárez, which is being pummeled by civil war. How relaxed, how nonchalant these spectators appear. Beneath their serene facade, some may have been waiting like vultures to pounce upon a dying prey, once they were

sure all the fight had left it. Indeed, residents of El Paso did share in looting Juárez, even to its churches, once Mexico's federal troops had formally surrendered to the rebel enemy.

Of course, revolution watching could be dangerous entertainment, and errant bullets claimed more than a few spectators.[13] Enough oglers fell to create suspicion that on occasion a spiteful Mexican deliberately pointed the muzzle of his rifle north. Yet Americans never tired of the spectacle. It was as if they believed that Mexican bullets could not kill them; perhaps they were flaunting a well-ingrained disdain toward Mexicans.

However foolhardy its pursuit, revolution watching was good for local business. El Paso's famous Hotel Paso del Norte offered its guests special rooftop viewing of the travail of Juárez, folding chairs perched on tables, undoubtedly with service of cocktails or beer.[14] A postcard writer, glad that his friends Lillie and John would soon visit him in El Paso despite the heat, sent them a wonderful picture card: ladies in long, white dresses, their fancy parasols and huge bonnets shielding them against a hot sun, saunter along a river bank which slopes toward the Rio Grande. Nicely dressed children wander through the scene. Most of the menfolk, in bowler hats and dark three-piece suits (although many have shed jacket and vest because of the heat), line the river bank; some women are with them. Across the river, not very wide at this point, more than one hundred insurgents cluster. No one seems to be crossing the river. The two groups look at each other, maybe socializing, perhaps shouting.

Some verbal exchanges across the boundary

were not very polite. When a black U.S. soldier went to the river to water his horse, a Mexican military man across the way called out in unconstrained English, "Hey Coon! When are you damned Gringos going to cross that line?" "Chili," came the response, "We ain't going to cross that line at all. We're just goin' to pick up that line an' carry it right down to the Big Ditch [Panama Canal]!"[15]

Farther west along the border, motorists drove from San Diego, California, to a bluff overlooking the 1912 battle of Tijuana. Photographed beside their cars, they appear as nonchalant as other border-watchers. Some viewers pitched tents for a camp-out but hurried home when the fighting flared and rebels retreated toward them from across the international line. One card sent all the way from California to Parris Island, South Carolina, said: "I wish you were here to see the sights." The postcard pictured a grizzled rebel soldier in battle dress, his marvelous face etched by the history of Mexico.

Among the most popular postcards were those that showed the burning bodies of Mexicans; huge, filled burial pits; gruesome lynchings and public executions in Ciudad Juárez. Entrepreneurs like Walter Horne printed and sold these kinds of cards by the thousands and helped to create and/or reinforce public sentiment about Mexicans and their revolution. Some senders were frank about their feelings: "All these greaser bandits ought to go to the same place [their graves]." Others were less pointed: "Just wanted you to see what's going on down here," as if Mexicans ordinarily murdered and maimed each other in the course of daily activity. On one card displaying a large pile of tangled Mexi-

can corpses, the writer commented, "This one taken during one of the 'Spicks' favorite squalls." American soldiers certainly had no respect for Mexicans either as military adversaries or as a people.

The messages of the average soldier reflected the biases of their superior officers. The army's chief of staff, Hugh L. Scott, believed of Mexicans, "Firmness is essential in dealing with all inferior races, and they must have perfect confidence in your word," while General James Parker argued for occupation on grounds "that the turbulent history of Mexico, only one ninth of whose inhabitants are of white blood, demonstrates that only a protectorate similar to that established over Cuba will ever insure to its inhabitants the blessings of peace and prosperity."[16]

Many postcard pictures, of course, did not feature the carnage of war, but rather captured a telling moment in the developing drama. In front of us on a card we have the leadership of the revolt, with Ciudad Juárez defeated and Díaz about to sail into exile. In El Paso, Madero and his coterie make ready for their triumphal march to the capital, but first the group pose for pictures that become postcards. They are crowded photos, thirteen people in one, eighteen in another, all men, no women. Unified by victory, they are not of one mind. Now that the dictator has been eliminated, can their goals be unified, or even reconciled? All are well dressed, very bourgeois looking; no campesinos appear. The Madero family predominates; besides the leader, Francisco, there are his father and brothers Raul and Gustavo. Men who held positions in the Porfirian political structure are also present, such as Venustiano Carranza. So are the newcomers to public attention who had made their mark as natural military commanders, men like Pascual Orozco, a muleteer and small property owner from Papigochic, and Pancho Villa, foreman of a railroad section crew and before that a known cattle rustler. Their leader, Francisco Madero, appears small and frail; by comparison with the others he seems curiously comfortable and at ease, especially for a person assuming command of a troubled nation bounded by an anxious neighbor.

•

Madero's military struggle ended too quickly for his own good and that of Mexico. Madero and most everyone else underestimated the variety and strength of the social forces unleashed by the revolution. He lacked sufficient opportunity (and, some now insist, the intention and will) to consider the crucial issues raised by his former allies before they became adversaries and took up arms against him. He overtaxed the patience of Emiliano Zapata on land questions and frustrated the aims of unionized factory workers in Puebla. Nepotism evident in his appointments disgusted former loyalists like Pascual Orozco and Emilio Vásquez Gómez, and his entire approach to the country's future was much too conservative for the radical liberals. Finally, the rank and file soldiers who had made his victory possible wanted to be rewarded for their services. Admittedly, thousands of them were latecomers to the cause—individuals who joined only after they sensed triumph, but Madero offered them a pittance and told them to go home to their subsistence farms. Most refused to return. They had fought for gain and meant to obtain it. Madero counseled patience and made promises; desired reforms would be forth-

coming, but through recognized legal procedures. Few believed him and others could not wait. Even before he became president officially in November 1911, his former allies had become enemies, charging that he had betrayed the revolution.[17]

Armed struggle ensued almost everywhere: Zapata in Morelos, Vázquez Gómez and Orozco in Chihuahua, the radicals in Baja California, and countless unaffiliated bands which as yet waved no political banners but were determined to improve their lot. Bandits, too, turned out—to pillage in the name of social justice.

Madero intended to institute some desired reforms, but first he chose to restore public order, relying on the old Porfirian army (minus its high command). Although the move further rankled the opposition, it had some military success. His General Victoriano Huerta pushed Orozco into exile in the United States, while other federal units crushed the radicals in Baja California. Zapata's movement flourished but was contained mainly in Morelos and Puebla. The former Porfirian general and governor, Bernardo Reyes, once considered the logical successor to Díaz, tried (with the support of politically powerful Texas Mexican-Americans and perhaps the Texas governor himself) to mount a counterrevolution from Texas, but was captured in northern Mexico and imprisoned in the nation's capital. The country hardly enjoyed domestic tranquility, in spite of Madero's push in that direction.

Beneath the outward movement toward peace, various conspiracies against the regime struggled to acquire a successful mix of personnel and opportunity. In February 1913 a rebellion of military units gained a toehold in Mexico City itself. It stalled, however, until the very general that Madero trusted to quash the revolt, Victoriano Huerta, defected to the enemy with his troops and artillery. Huerta placed the incredulous Madero under house arrest, and the execution of the president and vice-president quickly followed. It was a bold coup indeed, made much more possible by the connivance of the U.S. ambassador to Mexico, Henry Lane Wilson.

Wilson had never trusted Madero to protect American lives and property. He disliked Madero personally—thought him weak and sniveling—and therefore undermined his administration whenever he could. Whether Wilson participated in the wanton assassinations of the nation's leading executives is not known. The rural police officer who actually pulled the trigger has been positively identified, but the question remains: who gave the orders?[18]

Huerta's betrayal rekindled the Mexican Revolution. The tragedy gave common cause to disparate groups (not all, for Pascual Orozco allied himself with Huerta) that aspired to avenge Madero and remold Mexico to their interests.

U.S. President Woodrow Wilson was aghast at the new developments below his southern border. Wilson's idealism encompassed world peace, democracy, and brotherhood; his model for achieving those admirable goals also happened to suit the interests of his country. Wilson's approach to foreign affairs embodied free enterprise (capitalism) and self-determination (democracy) as the means to world harmony and prosperity. He was so confident that his ideals were universal, and not simply peculiar to one culture or another, that he resolved to teach them whenever appropriate and possible. Mexico became the former professor's classroom,

but the Mexicans proved to be skeptical and unruly pupils.

A determined teacher, Wilson hardly spared the rod. He had at his command powerful tools, such as embargoes and loans, diplomatic pressures, the threat of intervention, and, if necessary, outright invasion. Wilson insisted that harsh, temporary means would yield salutary ends. Such obvious and unresolved contradictions in his thinking and policy doomed Wilson's program for Mexico. With the benefit of hindsight, it seems that the Mexicans did the teaching. Whether Wilson, and Americans in general, learned from the experience is another question.[19]

The usurper Huerta, president of Mexico following the martyrdom of Madero, became Wilson's main target. Huerta had to be removed and free elections held. Many Mexicans agreed; the downfall of Huerta became the cause that loosely linked myriad groups of Mexicans who hoped to steer the rebellion in their favor. While Huerta remained in power, these divergent interests entered an uneasy pact with Venustiano Carranza, who had proclaimed himself first chief of the Constitutionalists. Beneath the Constitutionalist veneer they were Zapatistas; Villistas; partisans of Lucio Blanco, or of Manuel Peláez, who patrolled Tampico and its vital oil reserves; followers of the politically ambitious Alvaro Obregón of Sonora, or of many, many other powerful, self-proclaimed chieftains. Most of their names have been lost to history or relegated to second rank because they were killed, reduced to submission, or satisfactorily rewarded by the eventual victors of the revolution.[20]

Huerta proved a formidable enemy. He reorganized and modernized the federal army and introduced political and social programs to broaden his base of support. He negotiated with foreign powers, specifically Germany and Japan, that could buffer him against (while at the same time intensifying the hostility of) the United States.[21] Huerta's enemies were implacable and increasing. Lucio Blanco won Matamoros for the Constitutionalists and unexpectedly initiated land reform.[22] Villa swept Chihuahua, eliminating Pascual Orozco in the process.

Pancho Villa took Ciudad Juárez literally like the Trojans took Troy. He forged a telegraph message to the federal commander there, saying that a relief train would arrive soon with sorely needed weapons and ammunition. The train arrived right on schedule, its boxcars filled with Villa's troops who quickly subdued the astounded federal garrison. Villa forced the major federal contingent in the state to seek refuge in the United States via Ojinaga.[23]

Villa's military exploits; his ebullient, if erratic, and earthy character; plus his general amicability toward Americans, including the Wilson administration, made him highly popular on both sides of the border. He loved to have his picture taken, and the producers of postcards eagerly obliged. When he directed his army toward the important federal stronghold of Torreón, he invited motion picture cameramen along to record the action. He even staged some battle sequences at their request. Villa posed before Torreón and then captured the city.[24] Meanwhile, rebel chiefs Alvaro Obregón and Plutarco Calles started in Sonora and began a long, hard campaign down the west coast of Mexico, and Zapata continued to tie down federal forces in Morelos.

Still, given the uncertainty of Mexican politics, the outcome of this struggle was by no means inevitable, and the president of the United States was an impatient man. He suffered frequent digestive discomfort and, while enduring it, might pat his stomach and quip: "Turmoil in Central America."[25] Mexico was giving him more than a stomachache, and he mustered all the moral and diplomatic pressures he could against the Huerta regime. His lofty determination to teach Latin Americans "to elect good leaders" led to the threat that if Mexican leaders did not "act together, and . . . act promptly for the relief and redemption of their prostrate country," the United States would find means "to help Mexico save herself and her people."[26] He also twisted the embargo spigot, permitting the shipment of war goods to those whom he preferred and shutting down the flow to others.

A sizable portion of the U.S. Army remained on the border. This pleased the military preparedness supporters, who had vehemently attacked both the president's reluctance to upgrade the army and his diplomatic watchful waiting. Mobilization allowed the military to test new equipment, such as its first air squadron, under the conditions of war alert. The policy also served those who urged the active protection of American lives and property, even to armed intervention. Some of Wilson's ranking advisors, including cabinet members, held extensive property interests in Mexico at the time.[27]

Although certain about Huerta's departure from office, Wilson was much less sure whom he should support as the Mexican president's replacement. He had hoped that Huerta would retire voluntarily, call for elections, and stay out of the race, but Huerta clung tenaciously to his presidency. In casting about for a suitable successor to support, the U.S. president favored a strongman who could guarantee the domestic peace and his countrymen's interests; no such person had yet emerged from the morass of rebellion. There was also concern about the direction of the revolution. Wilson and his business-minded cohorts wanted to ensure that it did not go too far—meaning that it not become truly social.[28] Mexican rebel chiefs continued their political jockeying, subordinated only to the ostensible desire to oust Huerta, and Wilson found an unexpected pretext to help them—at least one of them, Venustiano Carranza, who was among the most conservative of the lot.

The episode began on April 9, 1914 at Tampico, where the navy was showing the flag to ensure U.S. oil interests. A handful of U.S. sailors were arrested when they unwittingly landed for supplies in a zone considered militarily sensitive by Huerta's forces. It was a mistake on both sides, quickly rectified by Mexican authorities who released the errant landing party. But the American naval commander demanded that the Mexicans hoist an American flag in a prominent place of the city and render it a twenty-one-gun salute. The Mexicans naturally demurred, and Wilson had his opening. The invasion and occupation of the Caribbean port of Veracruz by American troops quickly followed.

The timing seemed especially right. A German ship, headed for Veracruz with arms for Huerta, was intercepted and prevented from entering the harbor. The ship moved south down the coast to unload its cargo, but the point was made. Furthermore, Mexico's major customshouse, a vital source of national revenue, lay in Veracruz. The United States had become deft at policing its Caribbean interests, including the new Panama Canal, by forcibly taking over the customshouses and managing the revenues of supposedly unstable, but definitely defenseless, countries within its self-defined sphere of influence. U.S. sailors and marines battled into Veracruz on April 21, 1914 and did not leave until November 23 of that year, more than four months after Huerta's departure for exile in Brooklyn. American apologists explained that the invasion had benefitted Mexico; it had, they boasted, greatly improved sanitary conditions in Veracruz.[29] The occupation also improved the picture postcard business. Ships had their own photographers, and boring months in Veracruz gave the soldiers plenty of time to write home.

•

A large group of picture postcards depicts the Veracruz affair. Some of them appear at the end of this section. The images are unabashedly patriotic, even jingoistic.[30] The stars and stripes appear everywhere: on the landing barge, raising the colors on the battlewagons, flying proudly over the occupied city, draped over the coffins of fallen men, on parade in New York City as the bodies are brought back home and paraded down the main thoroughfares. The messages on the cards convey the spirit of the moment: "Here's what made the Mexicans rave, seeing our ensign [flag] over the city. And it still hangs there. Wish they would try and take it down. There would be some fun." The sailors and marines did think killing Mexicans good sport: "This is a picture of two of our sailor boys and a dead Mexican that was killed by them. And we were not sorry to do it." On a card showing Mexicans engaged in street fighting against the invaders, another American soldier wrote, "These are the umbries [hombres?] we were fighting. These fellows were fighting us when these [photos] were taken. Don't think many are telling the story now." On a card with sailors posed like triumphant hunters over the bodies of several Mexicans, the message is simple: "Some of the lanky boys in blue, and some of their work."[31]

A photo of American militarymen in the middle of a wide open street, firing their machine guns and rifles at an unseen enemy off to the right: the writer asks and then answers, "Do they look afraid? I guess not." Dead Mexicans are shown sprawled in front of the Hotel Diligencia, while marines stand over them, rifles pointed at the corpses. Other Americans pose in the foreground of a photo, seated confidently on two baggage dollies, while in the background lie three dead Mexicans, civilians dressed in the simple white cotton clothing of common people. The sender wrote: "Here is one place my company did some execution. There were about 25 men fighting from around this place. Mostly civilian."[32]

On the quarterdeck of the U.S.S. *Louisiana,* sailors and marines are in rank ready for landings in Mexico. The sender writes: "A picture of the company I was in. I have myself marked. Do you think it looks like your baby? Just going ashore to kill Mexicans." An inked arrow designates the tiny image of a sailor in line. Under a magnifying glass, a smallish, baby-faced boy looks straight at the camera, which is above him, on another deck, and quite far away.

Somber messages, but occasionally mixed with mirth, appear on other postcards sent by the troops at Veracruz: "Dear Wife, Just in from a funeral. Capt. Owens, U.S.M.C., died here night before last. All the Marines turned out for the funeral. His body comes back to the States on the U.S.S. Florida. They took moving pictures of us so I am a movie actor now. Maybe by the time I get back I will be able to see my own movie picture." Another card pictures an attractive park in central Veracruz, its garden designs visible and white-clad U.S. sailors sprawled everywhere under the palms: "This is a park that was just across the street from the barracks that we were quartered in. In this park we washed and dried our clothes. And we slept afternoons and fooled with the Mexicans girls when we were not on duty. We also got a lot of coconuts off the trees." And finally an interesting three-story building obviously built for a tropical ambiance with its airy, arched entrances and balconies across the entire front decorated with simple, wrought-iron railings— it is the Salón de Variedades, the civic theater of Veracruz. Art posters of Mexican entertainers still adorn the facade. Now it is headquarters for a U.S. naval contingent; the sailors' rifles are stacked, while the men mill around the front of the structure. A sailor writes: "This is the barracks we were quartered in while ashore. Here we slept right on the wooden floor and benches. Although we picked out the soft side of the boards."[33]

There is pride in the way the naval bombardment chewed out huge chunks of mortar from the customshouse and the naval academy, though marines complained that army troops dispatched to occupy the city after it had been captured tried to claim battle glory for themselves. A marine wrote on a picture of a bivouacked army unit: "This is some of the army that arrived a couple of weeks after we had the town. They didn't hear a shot, yet still to hear some of them talk, they took the city. But when we mention the 15th, 16th, or 17th company marines, they close up like clams."[34]

There was plenty of braggadocio on these postcards, to be sure, but no writer mentions that the citizenry defended its homes door-to-door, or how the teenage cadets training in the academy heroically resisted, giving their lives for the honor of their country. In other photographs the men play baseball, one ship's crew against another, and enjoy a swim in the ocean. Some wrote about being transferred to Guantanamo Bay, Cuba, or to Santo Domingo. The U.S. military seemed to have plenty of enclaves to occupy.

•

The occupation of Veracruz denied financial resources and matériel vital to Huerta as Villa, Obregón, and Zapata bore down on Mexico City. Huerta fled, and the victorious rebels occupied the capital. With Huerta deposed the Constitutionalist leaders assembled in Aguascalientes in October 1914 to plan the country's future. The immediate task concerned the selection of an interim president, pending elections. Carranza demanded the position; Villa and Zapata disagreed, and the convention collapsed into civil war. Undoubtedly a good many Mexicans welcomed the renewed fighting. For them the revolution meant much more than simply choosing a new leader; they had ideas and preferences about the way the nation should be run and for whose benefit. A good portion of the rebels aimed to remake society. Their strong convictions kept the fighting alive for several more years until the Carranza faction triumphed and stamped Mexico with its brand of bourgeois authoritarianism rooted in private enterprise.

The Wilson administration warily watched these events and wondered how it could force Mexico to put its house in order, a task deemed all the more urgent by the advent of war in Europe. Increasingly the United States appeared drawn against its will into the European conflict on the side of the Allies, and it became critical to secure the U.S. southern flank.

Germany, naturally, would have liked to keep the U.S. out of Europe's fight, or at least on the periphery of it. One way would be to embroil the U.S. in continuing conflict with Mexico. Outright war between the two countries would be preferable, and German agents agitated toward that end. Carranza understood the situation. He did not relish war with the United States, but he meant to drive a hard bargain with Wilson in exchange for Mexico's cooperation, or at least neutrality. If German intentions served his purposes, so much the better.[35]

Wilson's heightened frustration over Mexico's failure to learn his lessons and to follow his lead, coupled with Carranza's steadfast denunciations of U.S. interference in Mexican affairs, edged the two nations toward open conflict. To some it seemed that war between the neighbors was inevitable.

The Constitutionalists needed official U.S. recognition to gain legitimacy in Mexico, and to earn recognition, they had to control national affairs. They made important advances in that direction in 1915. First they virtually eliminated Villa as a battlefield foe with staggering victories over their rival in the spring. Villa ferociously hurled his cavalry at fixed positions guarded by trenches, barbed wire, and interlacing machine-gun fire. In the end, his ranks were decimated; his scattered command began to defect with units they controlled. Villa limped back to his lair in Chihuahua. Zapata's resistance remained virulent but contained in the state of Morelos, and U.S. authorities thwarted the renewed revolutionary attempts of Victoriano Huerta and Pascual Orozco by arresting the two leaders in El Paso. Clearly, although it did not like Carranza at all, the United States government leaned in his direction to bring stability to Mexico, which also meant controlling popular elements who favored radical change over limited reform.[36]

Clever, pragmatic, even cynical, Carranza hastened the recognition process by taking advantage of a rebellion centered around the bizarre Plan of San Diego (Texas), whose writers contrived to dismember the United States of all its Southwest and more. The Plan, dated January 6, 1915, called for a February uprising in the so-called diamond of Texas—along the border from Brownsville to Laredo—proclaiming Texas, New Mexico, Arizona, Colorado, and California as the independent homeland of Mexican-American, Japanese, Native Americans, and other racial minorities. Six states contiguous to this Mexican-American republic (Arkansas, Oklahoma, Colorado, Nevada, Louisiana, Oregon) would be given to blacks. All Anglo males in the area over sixteen years of age would be slain.

Marauding under a red and white flag emblazoned with the legend "Equality and Independence," the rebellion began on schedule on February 20, 1915.

For the first few months the revolt was limited to cattle rustling, ranch raiding, and hit-and-run skirmishes with federal soldiers and Texas Rangers. But by July the mayhem had begun in earnest: bridges burned, stores looted, a train derailed, and its Anglo passengers robbed. Raiders forayed northward to attack a subheadquarters of the reknowned King Ranch, while enlarged parties of rebels openly battled troops of the U.S. cavalry and the Rangers with heavy casualties on all sides. The insurgents even sniped at military patrol aircraft attempting to chart their movements from overhead. No longer confined to Mexico, civil war invaded south Texas with a vengeance.[37]

The wanton viciousness of these Texas episodes was more than matched by the reprisals of Texas Rangers ordered to restore public peace at whatever cost. The "Rinches" loved to bully and beat residents of the region, almost all Mexicans or Mexican-Americans and the great majority of them innocent of any complicity in the Plan of San Diego. The *Washington Post* reported that any Mexican (-looking person) found armed was "under instant suspicion. If he is slow to explain, his life is in immediate danger; and if he makes any threatening move, his life is forfeited."[38] Indeed, a Ranger captain summarized his day's activities: "We got another Mexican, but he's dead."[39] A new verb gained prominent usage in the region: "rangered."

Mexican-Americans were being "rangered" to death. Picture postcards recorded the brutality, as Rangers stood proudly over their dead victims. One dragged the corpses of his quarry through the spiny mesquite brush and then apparently photographed them himself for postcard purposes. Evidently, he intended to send them to friends. The *San Antonio Express* even grew tired of the scene and reported that the finding of dead Mexicans "has become so commonplace" that "it created little or no interest."[40]

In all, the year 1915 recorded seventy-three separate raids in the valley, many in the name of the Plan of San Diego. Some 25 Anglos and perhaps 150 or more Mexicans and Mexican-Americans died. Ranger violence led to the death of hundreds more (some say thousands) Mexican-Americans. The violence halted economic activity for a year, and an estimated one-half of the terrified Mexican-American population migrated to Mexico, never to return.[41]

In the aftermath, the *Laredo Times* editorialized that the troubles "indicate that there is a surplus population down there that needs eliminating."[42] To Texas Governor James E. Ferguson, "The problem with the Texas-Mexican population is that their sympathies are with Mexico, and they never extend any cooperation to our authorities but are continually aiding and abetting the lawless element overrunning our country from Mexico."[43]

What was the bloodshed all about? The answer is not yet entirely clear. Mexican-Americans residing in south Texas had sufficient grievances at the time of the Plan of San Diego. Whether or not they would have welcomed political independence is debatable; some of them undoubtedly took advantage of the unrest created by the plan's backers to settle personal accounts with power-brokers and

others. German agents and adherents to Carranza also took advantage of the chaos to further their own concerns vis-à-vis U.S.-Mexican relations. Until the turn of the century south Texas was primarily cattle country, largely devoid of water and transport. In 1904 a railroad into the valley made farming feasible; irrigation would make it profitable. Anglos caught the scent. Speculators and farmers filtered into the region, bought up the cheap land, and began to irrigate. Very profitable agriculture was indeed possible, but a good deal of land, especially acreage close to the Rio Grande, was owned by or had been worked for generations by Mexican-Americans, descendents of people who had resided there since the Mexican War, or by Mexicans who had taken advantage of loose immigration policies to swim the river and settle down.[44] Continuing unrest along the border heightened by the revolution and made especially violent by the Plan of San Diego made the displacement of settlers by aggressive Anglo business interests just that much easier and much more probable. An understanding of land tenure before and after the horrid events of 1915 may more fully illuminate the motives played out during the entire affair.

We can identify at least one victor emerging from the tragic Plan of San Diego: Venustiano Carranza. It was well known at the time that Carranza's soldiers participated in the raids. Certainly, the Constitutionalists furnished weapons and ammunition to the rebels. Carranza's agent in Washington, D.C., informed the U.S. government that once Carranza was diplomatically recognized, the raids would cease, which is precisely what happened. Wilson's government rendered Carranza *de facto* recognition on October 19, 1915, and south Texas settled down.[45]

This news fell on some particularly sensitive ears. By the fall of 1915, Pancho Villa, Carranza's old rival, had partially reconstituted his army and planned to recoup popularity and power with a campaign through Sonora. His first target was the border town of Agua Prieta, opposite Douglas, Arizona. Villa was approaching the town with massed cavalry when told of Wilson's choice for leader of Mexico. He was furious, and understandably so. Of all the Mexican chieftains, Villa had been the most friendly toward, and most cooperative with, the United States. He had not denounced the landing at Veracruz, and he had tailored border battles so that fewer bullets fell in the United States. Now Uncle Sam had turned on him. Furthermore, he may have suspected that Carranza had bargained away special privileges, even national territory, in a deal for diplomatic support.[46]

An extremely angry and dangerous Villa unleashed his forces against Agua Prieta. The Constitutionalists were ready, reinforced by troops that Wilson had allowed to be hurriedly ferried by train across the southern United States to ensure their presence at the confrontation. Villa attacked at night, as usual, but gigantic searchlights fed by electricity from Douglas illuminated his maneuvers. Once again his horse troops capitulated to modern warfare; trenches, barbed wire, and coordinated machine guns delivered him a decisive defeat.[47] Pancho Villa swore revenge on the United States.

Serious labor strife marked increasing ferment and discontent in Mexico soon after the turn of the century. Copper miners at Cananea, near the Arizona border, struck in 1906 for better wages and improved working conditions. Violence flared; arson and murder resulted. The drama was best captured on a series of photo postcards. Here the mob weighs its action before the hated company store at the American-owned enterprise. (Courtesy Library of Congress.)

American vigilantes bent on revenge soon arrived at Cananea, among them professional people, ne'er-do-wells, lawmen, and businessmen. Some later swore they also saw Arizona Rangers and U.S. soldiers among the group. There they stood, eyeball-to-eyeball, the Americans defending the company's property, the miners threatening to destroy it. Mexican *rurales* and soldiers eventually restored order, but the international incident severely shook the Díaz dictatorship and encouraged further unrest along the border. (Courtesy Library of Congress.)

Francisco I. Madero, idealistic and legalistic, stubborn and wealthy, in 1910 proclaimed the revolt against the aged dictator, Porfirio Díaz, who had, through compromise and brute force, ruled Mexico for nearly three decades. Characteristically, the rebel leader appeared for photographers in his tan whipcord Norfolk jacket, riding breeches, and smart English boots. Madero's cause attracted energetic political journalists, like Juan Sánchez Azcona, and ordinary countrymen, such as small landholders from the Valley of Papigochic in western Chihuahua, including José de la Luz Blanco, who became one of Madero's first generals. (Courtesy Andreas Brown Collection.)

No. 1 Francisco I. Madero, Jr. No. 2 Francisco Madero, Sr. No. 3 Dr. Vázquez Gómez. No. 4 Abraham González. No. 5 Señor Carranza. No. 6 Guadalupe González. No. 7 Lic. José M. Pino Suárez. No. 8 ____ Mayotorena. No. 9 Alberto Fuentes. No. 10 Gen. Pascual Orozco, Jr. No. 11 Juan Sánchez Azcona. No. 12 Alfonso Madero. No. 13 José de la Luz Blanco. No. 14 Lic. F. González Garza. No. 15 José Garibaldi. No. 16 Raul Madero. No. 17 Gustavo Madero. No. 18 Pancho Villa.

Sensing their triumph over Díaz, the rebellion's leaders (provisional president, some provisional governors, military commanders, and peace commissioners) posed for this group photo on April 30, 1911. It was the closest they ever came to being together about anything. Vázquez Gómez and Pascual Orozco were soon in outright rebellion against Madero, charging that he had betrayed the revolution. Pancho Villa and José de la Luz Blanco defeated him on the battlefield, and others pictured here, including family members, became members of his brief and turbulent administration. (Courtesy Andreas Brown Collection.)

The revolution also attracted a number of foreigners, mostly from the United States: filibusters, soldiers of fortune, adventurers. Some were well paid for their expertise as machine gunners or dynamiters. Others fought for the fun of it, and even a few for political convictions, some of them much more radical than those of their leader. (Courtesy John Hardman Collection.)

Garibaldi

The most heralded member of the foreign legion, Lieutenant Colonel José Garibaldi, grandson of the unifier of Italy, participated in the May 1911 assault on Ciudad Juárez and received the defending federal commander's sword in surrender. (Courtesy El Paso Public Library.)

WATCHING THE FIGHT IN JUARES, FROM EL PASO.

Revolution-watching from the U.S. side of the border became a favorite spectator sport. Of course, it could be dangerous; during firefights bullets zinged in all directions, and some may even have been deliberately aimed at the spectators. As a result, a good many Americans died, creating sharp, high-level diplomatic exchanges, even to the threat of war. U.S. Army soldiers tried to keep the crowds behind barriers a reasonable distance from the battle sites, but stray missiles continued to claim their victims. In later reports to the U.S.-Mexican Claims Commission, Americans asked damages for their losses. They testified that they were innocently pursuing their daily lives when injured by a Mexican bullet. In fact, most were hurt while gawking at battle scenes from a dangerous perch. (Courtesy Andreas Brown Collection.)

AMERICANS AND INSSURECTOS AT RíO GRANDE

A participant remembers: "A lot of people would go alongside the river and watch the fighting. They would stand and watch like damn fools. They killed a little boy who was standing right close to me. He got hit and started crying, and I knew goddamn well he got hit! Deader than hell, a little boy about six or seven years old, standing there and watching them. And them goddamn people wouldn't get out of the way . . . ." (Courtesy Andreas Brown Collection.)

Ciudad Juárez was battered by the rebel attack. Dynamiters burrowed through the insides of buildings to avoid fire from federal machine guns which strafed the long, narrow streets from fixed and fortified positions. After a truce had been called, curiosity seekers and looters arrived from El Paso to inspect the damage and to partake of the spoils. (Courtesy Carter Rila Collection.)

Identifying Dead Federals and Collecting them for Burial.

As proved to be true for the entire revolution, the early fighting was ferocious; no holds barred. Capture usually meant public execution, and, to avoid it, thousands opportunistically switched allegiances. A celebrated novelist Mariano Azuela, captured the senselessness: " 'Why do you keep on fighting, Demetrio?' Demetrio frowned deeply. Picking up a stone he threw it to the bottom of the canyon. Then he stared pensively into the abyss, watching the arch of its flight. 'Look at that stone; how it keeps on going . . . .' " (Courtesy Nita Stewart Haley Memorial Library.)

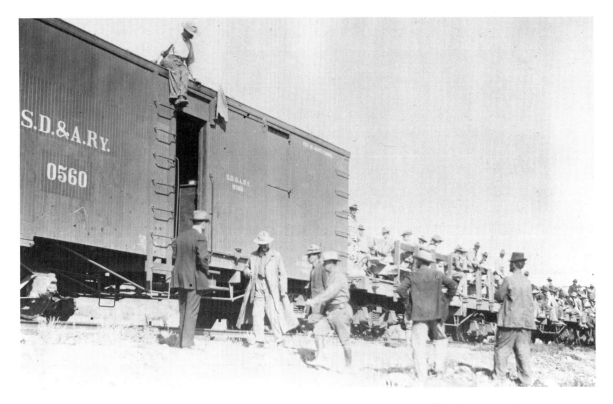

Even as Madero maneuvered to consolidate his victory, political liberals in Baja California mounted a challenge which aimed to radicalize the rebellion. They hijacked a train at San Diego, California, and headed for Tijuana. Dan Armstrong, the conductor, was taken prisoner but was released when the rebels were finished with the train. (Courtesy San Diego Historical Society.)

San Diegans flocked to the border in a variety of conveyances to witness the impending battle of Tijuana and piled up at the customshouse to await the outcome and the opportunity to see, and in some cases to loot, the remains. The rebel leader Ceryl Pryce, who needed funds for ammunition and provisions, encouraged the tourist trade. He charged visitors 25¢ to see the village, and placed a 25 percent tax on receipts at its gambling houses. (Courtesy San Diego Historical Society.)

Gen. Price.
Commanding the rebels
at Tijuana 5/9-1911.

Ceryl Ap Rhys Pryce, a Welch free-lance soldier who had formerly served British imperialism in Africa, commanded the radicals, whose ranks had been enlarged by dozens of Industrial Workers of the World from the United States. They attacked and took Tijuana with 220 men on May 9; 7 Americans and 25 Mexicans died in the fight. Rumors about the aims of the movement abounded: was Baja to be a free republic or perhaps annexed to the United States? The following month the Mexican federals counterattacked and forced the Liberals across the border where authorities arrested Pryce for violations of neutrality laws. Pryce, however, won acquittal, played a few bit parts as a cowboy hero in Hollywood films, won medals for service in the British army during World War I, resigned his rank of major in 1919, and soon disappeared from official records. (Courtesy Andreas Brown Collection.)

The Liberal army was a conglomeration of mostly young men in their makeshift khaki uniforms and cowboy outfits. Some claimed to be college students; others were veterans of the Boer War. Third from the left is Steve "Shorty" O'Donnell, an adventurer. They used the building in the background for a hospital. San Diego had been fairly tolerant toward organized labor before the events of 1911, when the speechmaking of "Splendid Emma" Goldman and that spirited singing of IWW anthems changed sentiments:

> Out there in San Diego
> Where the western breakers beat
> They're jailing men and women
> For speaking in the street.

All this inclined the city's civic leaders to the right, a posture maintained to this day. (Courtesy Ralph Bowman Collection.)

There were several battles of Tijuana before the Mexican regulars defeated the Liberal filibusters for good. Casualties were heavy on each side, and the Red Cross provided most of the field hospital services. Among the volunteers were some of San Diego's most distinguished citizens, including Dr. Harry M. Wegeforth (identified with the X), a physician and surgeon who had in 1910 come to the area from Baltimore. He is best remembered as the founder in 1916 of the famous San Diego Zoo. (Courtesy San Diego Historical Society.)

"Biding farewell to their Native Land"

Pancho Villa's defeat of the federal army at Ojinaga in January 1914 unleashed a flood of Mexican refugees into Texas. They were, in the main, soldiers, their families, camp followers, and others, rich and poor, from Chihuahua City, who feared the vengeance of Villa. The eight days that it took them to walk across the rocky desert and through mountain passes to the border exacted a tremendous toll in human suffering. A newspaper called the march "a spectacle of despair." After their stint in U.S. refugee camps, many decided not to return to their homeland. (Courtesy Edward McBride Collection.)

The sight of more than 5,000 refugees streaming into El Paso, even under U.S. military guard, alarmed the general citizenry. Would these unfortunates be allowed to join the already glutted local labor market? Would Villa attack El Paso to avenge any assistance given the refugees? How about disease and social disorder? Hugh Scott, the military commander in charge of the district, assured the local city council that the newcomers would be kept under heavy guard at nearby Fort Bliss in a tent camp surrounded by barbed wire and well lit at night. Besides, he noted, merchants would benefit from the $1,000 a day spent to provision the camp. (Courtesy El Paso Public Library.)

Mexican Refugees at Fort Bliss, Tex.
1103.

An El Paso physician warned: "They are aliens, civilians, indigent, unhygienic and liable to become public charges. In fact, they are obnoxious to every law governing the admission of aliens into the United States." (Courtesy Nita Stewart Haley Memorial Library.)

Typical Refugees
1105

The *El Paso Morning Times* countered: "The *Times* is glad to have this opportunity to voice as it feels it does voice, the practically unanimous judgement
of the intelligent and hospitable people of El Paso, that the presence of this
large number of citizens of Mexico is not a menace, but a source of prosperity and happiness to the people of this city." (Courtesy Library of
Congress.)

ON THE INSIDE LOOKING OUT
REFUGEE CAMP

Under public pressure "Uncle Sam's Guests" were transferred from the El Paso area to the more remote Fort Wingate in southern New Mexico. There they remained until April 1914 when the noncommissioned officers, privates, and their followers were released. In all, the military interned 5,296 ordinary Mexicans at Fort Bliss, including 1,237 women and 532 children. Wealthy refugees, such as the Luis Terrazas family, enjoyed a free run of elite El Paso society from the start. (Courtesy Library of Congress.)

MEXICAN FEDRALS FIGHT-
ING IN STREETS DURING
CAPTURE OF VERA CRUZ
BY AMERICANS, APR 1914.
-L⋅L Photo #3⅛

The American landing at Veracruz in April 1914 was unopposed by the Mexicans for the first few hours. Then a municipal gendarme, Aurelio Monffort, fired a single shot at a contingent of sailors crossing a street intersection. A fusillade followed. Civilian snipers and disparate military squads, some with automatic weapons and small-caliber artillery pieces, rallied to resist the invasion. Several days of heavy fighting followed. (Courtesy Andreas Brown Collection.)

KILLED ON CORNER OF M. LERDO AND MORELOS.   L & L Photo

This photo postcard shows the corner of Miguel Lerdo and Morelos streets, where Monffort first fired his rifle. U.S. troops advancing from the port's customshouse rolled forward the bags and barrels seen at the right for protection against Mexican rifle fire. The makeshift barricade did not shield them from rooftop snipers. (Courtesy Andreas Brown Collection.)

With Monffort dead along with his fellow defenders, the U.S. military secured the corner. Sailors especially liked to pose for photos at this site of their triumph. (Courtesy John Hardman Collection.)

At. Vera.Cruz.Mex. April.22.1914.

As Mexican resistance unexpectedly continued into the second day after the landing, new contingents of U.S. marines and sailors readied themselves to go ashore. A number admitted that they looked forward to the opportunity to kill Mexicans. As the landing parties passed several British cruisers anchored in the harbor, the English sailors cheered them on: "Give 'em hell, Yanks! Give 'em hell!" (Courtesy John Hardman Collection.)

Dying
Clothes.

Meanwhile aboard the U.S. battleships, men about to land, fearful that their white uniforms would make them easy targets for Mexican snipers, dyed them brown in vats of water colored by coffee grounds and in tubs of water drawn from their ships' rusty boilers. (Courtesy Carter Rila Collection.)

The Stars and Stripes were formally raised over Veracruz on April 27, 1914. Elsewhere in Mexico the flag was trampled and burned in protest. Mobs attacked the U.S. Embassy and various consulates along with businesses, hotels, and restaurants frequented by "gringos." At Monterrey the American consul was temporarily kidnapped, and everywhere American lives and property seemed endangered. (Courtesy Andreas Brown Collection.)

The U.S. Government had warned Americans in Mexico to leave long before
the troops landed at Veracruz, but many had refused to abandon the life into
which they had settled. However, repercussions of the events at Veracruz sent
thousands toward evacuation from the Caribbean port. Most who left lost
their small businesses and personal belongings to furious Mexicans and had to
accept Red Cross assistance in order to leave. In all, 60,000 Americans had to
evacuate Mexico. (Courtesy John Hardman Collection.)

funeral Parade of Bluejackets Brooklyn

© F.A.Toomb [...]

Armed intervention, of course, was bound to take its toll. President Wilson's advisors had assured him that there would be no bloodshed at Veracruz, but in the first day alone four died and twenty were wounded. "I cannot forget that it was I who had to order those young men to die," lamented the president. The bodies of the troopers were returned to the U.S. and paraded with pomp and circumstance down the nation's major avenues, such as this one in Brooklyn. Dignitaries, including cabinet members and the assistant secretary of the navy, Franklin D. Roosevelt, attended to pay their respects. (Courtesy Andreas Brown Collection.)

The U.S. Navy, and soon the Army, occupied the town and placed it under military control. The best buildings in town were commandeered as company headquarters and barracks. Apologists later justified the occupation with assertions that the troops brought honesty and efficiency to local government in Veracruz, established a decent school system, controlled prostitution and disease—got rid of the vultures that had literally feasted in the streets. (Courtesy Andreas Brown Collection.)

Destitute residents of Veracruz, largely women and children, appealed to the invaders for leftover scraps of food from their mess kits, along with clothing and supplies. And a few Veracruzanos profited: petty merchants who set up stalls to hawk their goods near the barracks of the soldiers, owners of restaurants, cantinas, and recreation halls, along with the producers and vendors of photo postcards. (Courtesy Andreas Brown Collection.)

Sailors at home. Vera Cruz '14

Mexican young ladies seemed to interest some military personnel mainly as cultural artifacts—at least, insofar as the men dared pose with them for picture postcards to be sent back home. (Courtesy Carter Rila Collection.)

A postcard cartoon reflects the naïvete (and some would add racism) of the U.S. militarymen. They thought the young ladies of Veracruz would resemble fair-skinned, flamenco-styled Spanish women. Instead, they encountered much darker, wide-hipped señoritas. American soldiers who had stormed Mexico's Halls of Montezuma nearly seventy years earlier had made the same mental error. Actually, this card has invited a good deal of further discussion. Is the Mexican woman courting or rejecting the sleeping sailor? She is saying "amo," which might be shorthand for "te amo"—"I love you,"—or "amo" could mean "master." But what is the American flag doing on the ground? Was it simply inadvertently dropped there? Or was it hurled down in defiance? Some Mexican women actually opposed the occupation with rifles. Just as difficult to resolve is the intention of the individual who drew the card—probably an American serviceman. Why place the flag on the ground at all? Picture postcards certainly can challenge as well as titillate the historian. Regardless of these issues, there is not much doubt about the attitude of many U.S. officials toward ordinary Mexican women. A Navy ensign, acting as a deputy provost marshal, handled the complaint of a cab driver who had picked up a female passenger from a house of ill repute and taken her to her destination, where she declined to pay for the trip. The judicial authority settled the dispute "to what appeared to be their mutual satisfaction by suggesting that the fare be taken out in trade." (Courtesy John Hardman Collection.)

As the occupation wore on, military life became increasingly routine, and the soldiers vented their gripes and frustrations in letters and postcards sent home. In this case, they assured family, friends, and relatives that duty in Veracruz was hardly a tropical vacation joy. One could not even go for a swim for fear of sharks—and they were right. (Courtesy John Hardman Collection.)

A week after the landing at Veracruz, two detachments of navy airplanes—five aircraft and four pilots—arrived on ships to support the mission. This marked the first U.S. military naval air mission against a foreign power. AB-3 Curtiss flying boats, like the one pictured here, flew regular missions over the city and harbor to observe troop movements and to search for mines. These planes could be catapulted into service, but the navy only had a few catapult ships, none of them at Veracruz. So this plane was secured to a boat boom rigged as a crane and swung over the side for its fifty-minute flights. (Courtesy John Hardman Collection.)

The navy soon established a rough landing strip on a beach south of the city, so that these AH-3 Curtiss hydroaeroplanes had an easier take-off and landing. They had both pontoons and retractable wheels. The aircraft reconnoitered road conditions and Mexican troop positions from less than 1,000 feet up, and by their presence warned the Mexicans that the U.S. military might march farther inland. One of these pusher biplanes was hit in its bamboo tail by rifle fire, the first mark of combat on a U.S. military plane. (Courtesy John Hardman Collection.)

MEXICAN WAR SERIES NO. 3

AMERICAN ARMY AVIATORS IN MEXICO DOING ACTIVE WAR SERVICE.
LEFT TO RIGHT: LIEUTS HERBSTER, McILVAIN, BELLINGER, SEUFLEN,
TOWERS, MUSTIN, SMITH, ENSIGNS DE CHEVALIER AND STOLZ.
(ONLY GROUP PICTURE IN EXISTENCE.)

The aviators, who were never much for military discipline and who were allowed by their superiors to set their own pace, struck this informal pose. (Courtesy Carter Rila Collection.)

Gen. Huerta

The object of official American scorn leading to the occupation of Veracruz, Mexico's President Victoriano Huerta, was forced into exile in mid-1914. Within a year he attempted a comeback from U.S. territory but was intercepted by U.S. authorities in El Paso. Huerta was jailed for violations of U.S. neutrality laws and died in 1916 while under house arrest. (Courtesy Carter Rila Collection.)

A U.S. immigration official met Pancho Villa: "The general was a chunky, powerfully built man with the slender legs of a horseman, tiny, close-set eyes almost buried in a round, full face, and a thin-lipped mouth overpowered by a heavy drooping black moustache . . . ." (Courtesy Carter Rila Collection.)

"He gave everybody trouble, but you could look him in the eye, and if he was a friend, fine; if not, you'd better watch yourself from then on." (Courtesy Ralph Downey Collection.)

P. OROSCO H.

Pascual Orozco, a small landowner and muleteer from the Valley of Papigochic, became Madero's principal military commander in the crucial state of Chihuahua during the initial phase of the revolution. Early on he took up the fight against the dictatorship, while other Mexicans held back and weighed their chances. Within half a year, he had triumphed. (Courtesy El Paso Public Library.)

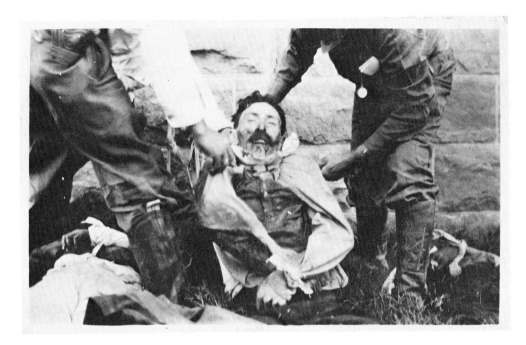

Disillusioned by Madero's presidency and influenced by counterrevolutionaries, Orozco rebelled against the chief-of-state and later joined the usurper, Huerta. With the arrest of Huerta in El Paso, Orozco fled into the mountains of the Texas Big Bend, where a posse hunted him down and killed him as a common cattle thief. Then they displayed his corpse for photographers to record. (Courtesy El Paso Public Library.)

Teenagers were swept into the revolution by the
thousands, and they fought for all sides in the
civil war; Villista, Carrancista, Orozquista, Fede-
ralista, it did not matter. The boys changed allegiances as casually as their more grown-up
counterparts. Because their youthfulness shielded
their intentions, the youths could infiltrate
enemy positions; they made good spies. If
caught, however, they were "adobed"—lined up
with other prisoners and shot. (Courtesy
Andreas Brown Collection.)

Some youngsters volunteered; others were force-drafted. A good many were orphans, drifters who craved food, attention, and adventure. (Courtesy John Hardman Collection.)

Macedonio Manzano, age fifteen, fought with the defenders of Matamoros against the Constitutionalists in 1915. His side lost, so Manzano was executed with other captives. (Courtesy John Hardman Collection.)

Border raids mixed with rumors of revolution among Mexicans and Mexican-Americans along the lower Rio Grande led the Texas Rangers to take reprisals. Hundreds of innocents died at the bloody hands of the "rinches." Thousands fled the valley into Mexico, never to return. The good land they vacated, much of it irrigated, was quickly occupied by American speculators and commercial farmers. (Courtesy John Hardman Collection.)

A victim speaks: "On one occasion the 'rinches' apprehended my cousin . . . right in front of our farm because they thought he was a bandit . . . . The 'rinches' then put my cousin in the [their] car and left. They took him to a cemetery about a block away, placed him in front of a cross and shot him dead . . . . The 'rinches' just apprehended people and took them. We were afraid to challenge them because they were like big animals and they had guns." (Courtesy Carter Rila Collection.)

Permanent headquarters of Mexican bandits in Hidalgo Co.

More testimony: "But the Rangers had established a precedent, that is, whenever a suspect was arrested they would unceremoniously execute him on the road to Brownsville or to jail, without giving him any opportunity. Frequently we would find dead bodies, and the ranches burned. Relatives were intimidated to the extent that they would not even bury their own relatives. That condition existed until it was nauseating, nauseating." (Courtesy Andreas Brown Collection.)

Adobe "Cook House" at Glenn Springs Tex.
in which 9 U.S. Soldiers made
their Def... Against Mexican Bandits

Some eighty Mexican raiders—one suspects that there were several Americans among them—attacked the settlements of Glenn Springs and Boquillas in the Big Bend in May 1916. They wanted guns, ammunition, and provisions. At Glenn Springs they encountered a detachment of eight U.S. soldiers. Six of the cavalrymen put up a sharp resistance from an adobe cookhouse, but the marauders burned them out, killing three. This challenge to the U.S. Army did not go unanswered. (Courtesy El Paso Public Library.)

Dapper George T. Langhorne, a well-to-do army major, led the chase of the Glenn Springs raiders in his chauffeur-driven Cadillac touring car. Two troops of the Eighth Cavalry followed, along with reporters, photographers, and two motion picture cameramen in two Ford sedans. Their "hot pursuit" carried them into Mexico. (Courtesy John Hardman Collection.)

The raiders commandeered a truck and several prisoners at Boquillas; when the truck bogged down in mud, the prisoners asked their captors to help with the pushing. When the Mexicans obliged, the Americans jumped them and captured their guards, including Lieutenant Colonel Navidad Alvarez (left), one of the bandit leaders. (Courtesy Andreas Brown Collection.)

Funeral possessions for U.S. soldiers killed on border duty became more commonplace. (Courtesy John Hardman Collection.)

Following devastating defeats in central Mexico in the spring of 1915, Pancho Villa meant to make a comeback at the border town of Agua Prieta, opposite Douglas, Arizona. En route he learned that the U.S. government had given official diplomatic recognition to his rival, Venustiano Carranza, and that the Americans had allowed the Constitutionalists to use U.S. railroads to reinforce the garrison at Agua Prieta. Villa fumed as he approached the border town where the Constitutionalists were ready and waiting. (Courtesy John Hardman Collection.)

"Greasers"

CARRANSA SOLDIERS COOKING TORTEAS AGUA PRIETA MEXICO

Americans had little sense of the issues in Mexico's civil war. Villista, Carrancista—to them, all Mexicans were "greasers" and were labeled as such on their postcards. (Courtesy Carter Rila Collection.)

Revolution-watching from Douglas, getting up high for a better view as Villa massed his cavalry for the attack. (Courtesy Special Collections, University of Arizona Library.)

Before the battle, U.S. soldiers relaxed in the trenches they had dug to defend themselves against errant missiles. They were also on military alert in the event that a "police action" was ordered for south of the international line. (Courtesy Special Collections, Research Library, University of California, Los Angeles.)

VIEW OF FORTS AGUA PRIETA

Villa hurled his cavalry at fixed gun positions protected by barbed wire and interlacing machine gun fire. The attackers were decimated; Villa blamed the Americans and vowed revenge. (Courtesy Special Collections, Research Library, University of California, Los Angeles.)

Is this really Pablo López? López, a Villista, was responsible for the wanton murder of fifteen American miners in January 1916 at Santa Isabel, Chihuahua. Whether Pancho Villa himself ordered the "gringos" hauled off a train taking them to their enterprise and shot is not certain. López was betrayed, captured, tried, and executed in June by the Carrancistas. His last wish was that all American spectators be removed from the public execution site. This was done. So now this postcard: American soldiers would be anxious to pose with the corpse of Pablo López. After Villa, he was the number two "most wanted." Yet Mexicans insist that no Americans were permitted at the execution, even less to touch the body of López. Did the most enterprising of all postcard entrepreneurs, Walter Horne, deliberately pose the photo with a substitute corpse? Horne would not have been beyond it. But debate over the identification of the corpse continues. (The authors of this book find corroborating photographic evidence persuasive but inconclusive. The body only seems to be that of Pablo López.) (Courtesy Carter Rila Collection.)

Chapter Four

Revenge and Reprisal

Despite the nighttime defeat at Agua Prieta some months earlier, Pancho Villa still preferred to attack at night under cover of darkness. It was about 3 A.M. on March 9, 1916 when he invaded the United States at Columbus, New Mexico. With some 450 horsemen he crossed the international boundary just west of the squat little border town (population 700), cut communication lines, split his troops and simultaneously attacked the center of town and its military outpost, Fort Furlong, a tent camp on the southern outskirts. The Villistas knew where they were going. In the aftermath of the incident, Americans realized that the strangers seen wandering about town the previous day must have been Villa's spies.

Tactically speaking, Villa circumvented the military sentries on duty at the border gate and caught the town literally asleep. His surprise was all the more complete because the military had received

only sketchy reports of his movements north from central Chihuahua, and the fragments of information put him at different points along the border at the same time. One report had Villa approaching Columbus but then veering off to the southwest. In response, the commander at Fort Furlong sent a contingent to a vulnerable ranch fourteen miles west of town, leaving some 350 men at the fort and another 67 at the nearby border gate itself.

Military leaders all along the border lamented the quality of intelligence about Mexican troop movements on the other side, but diplomatic caution in Washington precluded army excursions into Mexico for intelligence gathering or any other purpose. Nonetheless, Mexicans or Mexican-Americans hired by the U.S. as spies reported Villa nearing Columbus the day before the raid, and several said he intended to attack the town. In the official investigation that followed the sanguinary affair, the military cleared its command at Columbus of any unpreparedness; historians still examining the evidence have been much less kind.[1]

The Villistas—no eyewitness positively identified Pancho Villa himself among the marauders, but most people presume he was present—looted and burned the town and murdered a number of its inhabitants. Of the nine guests at the Commercial Hotel, five were murdered, one of them a Sunday school superintendent who had come to town for a conference. Across the street from the hotel, the raiders seized kerosene from a hardware store, doused nearby buildings, and burned them down. As might be expected, confusion cloaked everything. The Villistas seemed to have little more purpose than to shoot up the town and create mayhem, and maybe that is all they intended to do. As sharply awakened soldiers and civilians started to fire at the horsemen they saw silhouetted against the flames, bullets zinged in every direction.

The defense of Columbus was pretty much every man for himself. Officers, lodged with their families in homes scattered about town, found it virtually impossible to find their units in the confusion, let alone rally them for a coordinated counterattack. Nonetheless, the military men began to find their mark; Villistas dropped from their mounts. The army's response would have been much more effective had not one of its well-placed machine guns jammed almost immediately, the result of a misloaded cartridge container. Military experts argued later that the Benet-Mercier machine guns used at Columbus were a splendid weapon, light and fast-firing, though admittedly difficult to load properly at night. That explanation led the *New York Sun* to editorialize that the army's favorite machine gun "will answer the demands made of it between sun-up and sun-down, but it is not to be depended on after twilight."[2]

While raiders ravaged the main part of town, the second Villista column galloped into the rectangle of pitched tents called Fort Furlong. Only the cooks preparing breakfast and the stableboys tending the horses were awake. The cooks fought back with all they had—boiling water, potato mashers, carving knives, and the like; military reports assure us they did so effectively. Soldiers in varying stages of undress soon roused themselves to the challenge. They repulsed the Villistas trying to stampede the unit's horses, a turn of events that gravely cost the invaders. As dawn broke and the Villistas began to retreat into Mexico, the Americans mounted up and pursued them across the border, right into Chihuahua. There they exacted a terrible toll on the rear guard left by Villa to deter pursuit, while the main body of raiders headed south to safe haven in the Valley of Papigochic.

A body count after the fire fight showed that seventeen Americans had been killed in the attack, nine of them civilians. Six soldiers and one civilian were wounded. Among the raiders, sixty-seven were reported dead in Columbus itself, while some hundred more were said to have been killed during the pursuit into Mexico, a body count undoubtedly exaggerated by official military exuberance. The last total was not precisely verified because the Americans allowed the bodies of Mexicans to lie where they fell and let "those efficient Mexican doctors— the vultures—do the clean up."[3] The cleanup in Columbus attracted birds of different feathers.

Hardly had the Villista corpses been dragged from town to be burned than military reinforcements, newsmen, curious spectators, and, of course, photo postcard producers, including Walter Horne, arrived. They came by train and automobile from El Paso, sixty-five miles east, and down by road from Deming, thirty-one miles north, to survey the damage. To put it mildly, Columbus was astir as Americans debated how to react to Villa's challenge.

•

There were many postcard pictures of the aftermath of the attack. Several are shown at the end of the section. Villistas captured in the Columbus raid, pictured on this postcard,⁺ do not look like Mexican campesinos. They are well dressed; six of the eighteen wear somewhat disheveled dress jackets over their shirts. One quite elderly-looking man is distinguished by his white moustache, but the others are in their twenties or thirties, lean and fit. All hold their felt hats in front of themselves in semblance of submission, but soldiers guarding them probably told them to doff their hats for the picture. Their faces are resolute, a bit defiant, not at all downtrodden. One smiles as if to mock the photographer. They may have been captured, but they do not look defeated. The men are almost certainly all *norteños,* men of the north with few Indian features. (Perhaps they came from Papigochic, where inhabitants still boast of blue-blooded, direct descent from the Spaniards, even though they are largely racially mixed.) The photographic subjects later were tried by U.S. authorities for complicity in the Columbus raid. Seven were executed, three imprisoned, and the others exonerated and freed.

American soldiers loved to pose with their vic-tims—prisoners, wounded Mexicans lying on cots in front of a row of military tents, bodies collected for burning or in an open field. One postcard shows some Villistas on a funeral pyre about to be cremated. Curiously, also visible are the boots of two soldiers who must be standing on opposite ends of a bottom log in the pyre, as if to steady it for the picture, or at least to show a U.S. presence. On another card, an American cavalryman poses over the badly mauled corpse of a Mexican raider; the inference is that the trooper got his man. Such posed postcards proved to the public at large that their army was indeed at work on the border. Furthermore, there is no doubt how people who made the cards, and those who sent them, felt about the Villistas. They clearly labeled them in writing as bandits.

•

Why did Pancho Villa attack Columbus? Complex conspiracy or simple angry revenge, no one seems to know, but each observer with a favorite stance seems able to uncover supportive documentation. For those who find a German connection, Villa was prodded and assisted by German agents anxious to provoke an American reaction leading to open war with Mexico and thereby markedly reducing America's role in the European conflict. Others believe that without German connivance, Villa intended to provoke an American intervention to discredit his rival Carranza and encourage Mexicans to rally around Pancho Villa as their new national leader. The argument is that Villa had reason to believe that Carranza had traded his country's sovereignty for recognition. If he acquiesced in an American invasion, he would prove himself to be a tool of the U.S. If he resisted, his tie to Wilson would be ruptured. A more bizarre train of thought has Villa paid by the U.S. State Department to attack Columbus, giving the military a pretext to order the army into Mexico.[5]

Personal grievances also bear exploration as motives for the attack. One version says Villa paid a Columbus merchant for war goods which had not been delivered, and Villa went to collect the material and to punish the merchant who had reneged on the deal. It is entirely possible that no one owed Villa anything, but, following his long line of defeats, he was in desperate need of money, weapons, and ammunition for his beleaguered and dwindling army. Or did he think an attack on the United States would revive the morale of his troops?

A U.S. newspaperman, correspondent for the Associated Press, stands at the center of other accounts. The journalist, it is said, had secretly arranged for Villa to meet Woodrow Wilson in Washington, D.C., where the two of them could more directly discuss the so-called Mexican question. According to this rather fanciful thesis, Villa was not en route to the border to attack Columbus at all, but rather to meet with the contact who would escort him to the U.S. capital. Arrangements, however, broke down, and with the journey to Washington aborted, an infuriated Villa resolved to attack Columbus. When it comes to understanding Pancho Villa, you may have one partial truth, perhaps another; his aura, then and now, exercises the imagination.

Pancho Villa's motives were undoubtedly mixed, confused, complex, contradictory. His frustrations with the United States festered into an uninhibited hatred of gringos. As disasters, both diplomatic and on the battlefield, plagued this proud, arrogant, unpredictable, but often quite sensitive and emotional man, he must have blamed someone for his misfortunes, and with justification he could fault the United States. At any rate, he took out his anger on Americans.

In January 1916 (two months before the attack on Columbus) he had ordered a group of gringos to leave the Valley of Papigochic or be shot; they fled. Shortly thereafter, twelve American mining engineers and administrators were traveling by train to their enterprise in central Chihuahua when Villistas intercepted and killed them. Villa denied direct responsibility, but he received the blame. The sight of those bodies being returned to El Paso, where the men had families, friends, and relatives, caused a race riot in the Mexican quarter of that city. It took troops to restore calm and then to prevent an American posse bent on vengeance from crossing into Mexico.[6] None of this seemed to have changed the mind or the plans of Pancho Villa. He had told supporters in the Papigochic that he intended to invade the United States in order to punish Americans, and this is just what he did. En route he murdered some American farmers and ranch hands working in Mexico, perhaps more to shield his approach toward the border than out of spite, although later investigation showed that he was in a nasty, vengeful mood when he killed them.[7]

Villa's raid predictably inflamed U.S. public opinion. Americans, of course, resented any invasion of their territory, but the fact that a Mexican, and a man considered to be a bandit, had killed U.S. citizens on U.S. soil infuriated them. The kaiser was a foe, and Pancho Villa an insult. These attitudes became conspicuous as the Wilson administration pondered a response to Villa's provocation. The president considered Germany's intentions in Mexico. He weighed his nonintervention policy against his political future and then ordered Black Jack (originally Nigger Jack) Pershing to invade Mexico. The precise goal of the military campaign was muddled by Wilson's uncertainties over the entire venture, however. He told the press that Pershing had been told to "Get Villa!" When reminded that such a chase might carry the U.S. Army beyond Mexico, even to South America, the president reduced the mission to the scattering of Villa's forces. Pancho Villa himself was no longer the target.[8]

None of this was, as might be expected, palatable to Carranza, who insisted that his own army could, on its own, track down and punish Villa and his cohorts. An American presence was not welcome; in fact, if U.S. troops crossed the border, it could lead to war. Was Carranza bluffing? Wilson hoped so, but now he faced the fact that the Constitutionalists would not cooperate in a campaign against the Villistas. They would not let Americans use vitally needed railways and other communications lines; they would not guarantee daily provisions; they would render no intelligence data, no maps. And they might treat the expedition as an invasion and fight back.[9]

The U.S. military command considered all diplomatic considerations not germane to the situation a waste of time. American territory had been attacked, and the army meant to punish the invaders. Newspapers urged immediate action. "When, with almost the entire mobile army on the Mexican border," noted Omaha's *World Herald,* "it takes us a week to prepare to chase a 'second rate bandit in a third rate nation' the object lesson is so striking that nobody, even the extreme pacifists, can fail to be impressed by it." The *Duluth News Tribune* continued, "It is a fact that Germany can mobilize and put in action 1,000,000 men fully equipped from bandages to field kitchens in less time than the U.S. can get 5,000 men across the Mexican border."[10]

Pershing's punitive expedition of seasoned men, veterans of fighting in the Philippines and of border service, crossed the international line into Mexico on March 15, 1916. Only five weeks later the mission bogged down for good, hamstrung by Wilson's insistence that diplomatic negotiations precede military action, and tactically hampered by the rugged terrain and the hostility of the people among whom the cavalry units had to operate. More ominous, Mexicans were increasingly chafed by the intrusion of American soldiers into their civil strife, and so the United States and Mexico edged closer to open conflict.

Pershing commanded a supply train, plus companies of support troops and batteries of field artillery, some thirty-five miles south of Columbus, where he intended to establish field headquarters at a largely evacuated colony of U.S. Mormons near Casas Grandes. He ordered three flying columns of cavalry to the Papigochic region in pursuit of Villa. One of them, commanded by a cigar-chewing, ex-Indian fighter in his sixties named Colonel George A. Dodd, proceeded with daring, if not official authorization, to batter a main party of Villistas at Guerrero, the region's major town. He nearly captured Villa, who had been wounded in earlier combat but was evacuated as the Americans approached. This was the closest that the Pershing expedition ever came to catching its quarry, but no one is quite sure how close it really was.[11]

A second column under Colonel Frank Tompkins, who won the Distinguished Service Cross for his "hot pursuit" of the Villistas after the Columbus raid, rode south beyond the Papigochic to cut off the escape routes of the Villistas. They ended up at the southern Chihuahua mining city of Parral, a noted Villista stronghold with a population of some 20,000, now under the control of Carranza's troops. Military relations with the Constitutionalists there were frigid, and as the Americans resupplied themselves, paying for their goods with American dollars, the townspeople suddenly turned against them. Rocks and debris hurled at the gringos soon became bullets fired in earnest. As it was later explained, no self-respecting Mexican could permit a foreigner to capture Pancho Villa. A Mexican stated: "Villa has ravaged our ranches and looted our homes, but he started the blood rushing proudly through our hearts when he raided Columbus and defied the whole gringo army."[12]

Mexican soldiers caught the spirit, joined the wrathful mob, and increased its firepower. The Americans, numbering less than 100, retreated from Parral and realized just in time that they were headed for an ambush manned by several hundred of Carranza's troops. A sharp battle followed, with casualties on both sides. The Americans sent for reinforcements, and at this point it seemed that what had started as the pursuit of Villa would erupt into all-out war. But with a relief column of Americans approaching at a gallop, the Mexicans with-

drew, and a major engagement was avoided.[13]

The Carrancistas nevertheless accomplished more than they suspected; in effect, they had cut short the Pershing expedition. After Parral, Woodrow Wilson knew that Carranza—or at least some of his loosely controlled generals—would resist with force the U.S. invasion masquerading as an expedition.

The United States did not want war with Mexico, all the more so because Germany aspired and connived to promote just such a conflict. Therefore, while diplomatic negotiations with Mexico intensified, the Wilson administration ordered Pershing to consolidate his forces near his headquarters and to restrict his army's forays into the countryside. By this time, it had also become apparent that ranking U.S. government officials did not really care to capture Villa. Should they succeed, they wondered, what would they do with him?[14]

Serious thought given to withdrawing the expedition, however, ran into widespread U.S. opposition. "It makes the flesh of the American people run cold," claimed the *New York Press,* "to think that the Washington administration is capable of quitting in Chihuahua as it quit in Vera Cruz." And the *Birmingham Age Herald* echoed, "the American people will not tolerate the suggestion that the troops be withdrawn now, with the specious explanation that their work has been accomplished by scattering Villa's band. The orders say, 'Get Villa'." The Birmingham paper recalled Wilson's original pronouncement and intended to make him stick to it.[15]

Nor were the president's Republican foes any less relenting. Senator Henry Cabot Lodge declared

Figure 1.   Army recruitment poster for Los Angeles.

Figure 2.   Getting the boys in San Francisco to join up.

that, with the exception of President William Buchanan, no administration had subjected the U.S. to so much infamy "at home and abroad," while the inflammatory Senator Becon Fall, who had financial interests in Mexico, called Wilson "a pedagogue elevated to the presidential chair," who "has dealt with every crisis in a weak, mollycoddle, namby-pamby way that might be expected from a school teacher." He called Wilson's Mexican policy "one mistake after another," which "has increased the contempt of Mexicans for us." Fall disdained Mexicans even more than he did Wilson: "They can't fight. Look at those stupid little peons. After one glimpse of them you wonder no longer why Carranza's soldiers have never caught Villa."[16]

Fall predicted a Republican victory in November's elections, and Wilson feared he might be right. Electoral spectres were sufficient reason to keep the Pershing expedition in Mexico as long as he did—in all, eleven months—before they were quietly withdrawn. President Wilson also thought the continued presence of the expedition might pressure Carranza into cooperation, but Wilson thoroughly misunderstood and underestimated the Constitutionalist leader. The president should have at least recognized that Carranza's brand of nationalism held his movement together.

Finally, it has been argued that the expedition deliberately remained in Mexico so that the army could prepare itself for World War I, an assertion that remains to be proven. Military people might have seized such an opportunity; they would have welcomed involvement in Europe. But Wilson still saw a chance for a negotiated peace on the continent. Regardless of their respective intentions, the

mobilization and expedition permitted the army to test new equipment and to train personnel, to hone its command structure and modernize its supply and support services, for whenever and wherever they might be needed. Because of its Mexican venture, the U.S. Army finally became a twentieth-century fighting force, in large part due to Pancho Villa.

The Columbus raid gave the advocates of preparedness the wedge they needed to penetrate the national consciousness. Much of their bombast was part of an ongoing national feud, which was deeply rooted in national concerns and emotional issues involving pacifism, isolationism, and the role and responsibilities of the United States in world affairs. Villa tipped the balance toward military buildup. His assault not only propelled the Pershing expedition into Chihuahua but precipitated events which led to the mobilization along the border of the nation's entire national guard. It also advanced the National Defense Act of 1916, in which Congress, albeit with hesitation, agreed to budget an enlarged and modernized army.[17] *Current Opinion* wrote that neither the most colorful and vocal proponent of preparedness, Theodore Roosevelt, nor President Wilson on a speechmaking tour, could have accomplished what Villa did with Columbus: move a reticent Congress to act on behalf of the military.[18] In short, the so-called second-rate bandit from a third-rate country generated the pressure needed to propel the army into the twentieth century.

In the first place, the army became much more mobile, and supplies flowed more dependably as motor power replaced much animal power. The standard army vehicle at the time was the escort wagon, drawn by four mules; it could carry three thousand pounds of material. But its use presumed decent roads, and long trips required substantial forage. (The army needed sixty thousand pounds of grain and eighty-four thousand pounds of hay *daily* to feed its six thousand horses on the border.) In pack trains, each mule could carry only two hundred pounds, and forage remained a day-to-day hassle. Motor transport, on the other hand, had multiple advantages; it could operate twenty-four hours a day and rove farther from its supply base. Vehicles could carry sufficient gas and oil to fuel them for a week; no more daily forage. Also, truck convoys in comparison with animal transport required two-thirds less traveling space on roads, greatly reducing escort and security needs as well as opening up road space for other purposes. Finally, all this could be accomplished at less than half the cost of animal transport. Lobbyists for the cavalry had for some time resisted the military's efforts to motorize the army, and animal power was not at this time totally rejected, but Villa's raid shocked traditionalists and created an outcry for the rapid modernization of the military.[19]

Prior to 1916, the army had tested trucks but had not found a tough, practical vehicle suitable for military use. The Columbus crisis provided an ideal testing ground, and myriad makes of trucks, with varying capabilities, flowed to the border. First to arrive were twenty-eight White half-ton trucks—or at least the chassis of these vehicles. They came by train to Columbus, which became the depot for servicing the Pershing expedition. Once there, mechanics (airplane mechanics, because no truck mechanics were available) spent two days affixing wagon bodies to the chassis, so a hybrid truck/

wagon first saw service in Mexico. The War Department scoured the nation's manufacturers for additional vehicles but, finding none, ordered that two hundred trucks destined for France be redirected to the U.S. border. This bold and illegal official move skirted Congress, which had not funded the purchases, but Pershing needed trucks to supply his expedition. He got them, and Congress eventually caught up.[20]

By June 1916 the army possessed six hundred motor trucks—thirteen different types built by eight manufacturers—serving Pershing's headquarters in Mexico. And Mexico's roads provided some of the best tests anywhere. By the end of the campaign, the newly created truck corps had nine companies with twenty-seven trucks in each, its own regulations, and a table of organization.[21]

What the truck corps lacked were drivers and mechanics. Why recruit soldiers with such skills for an army that is not motorized? The army had to hire qualified civilians (some came with the trucks from the manufacturers) and pay them $100 a month, more than five times the amount earned by an infantryman on campaign. The wage differential naturally created a rivalry between the two groups; disdain for one another ill served the military mission. Tension heightened when the civilians, largely untrained in the use of small weapons, were issued rifles and pistols to protect themselves against Mexican hijackers. This friction eased only when the army began to train its own drivers and mechanics to replace the civilians.[22]

Trucks could be managed, but the deeply rutted dirt roads, which turned into quagmires in rain, defeated army attempts to use motorcycles. Despite the romance of their combat potential and the unquestionable daring of their drivers, military motorcycles, with machine guns mounted on their armored sidecars, simply could not negotiate the ruts and chuck holes in the risky roadways. When motorcycle gunners emptied their automatic weapons at targets, they sprayed the entire countryside with bullets. Given the circumstances, the motorcycle corps was relegated to minor communications duties and to military show, all on the U.S. side of the line.[23]

Passenger autos also served the military in Mexico. Seventy-three of them, mostly Dodges, but also Fords, Chevrolets, Studebakers, and Oaklands, were sent to the border; some wealthy officers brought their own customized vehicles to the frontier. Pershing had three cars, one rented from a local Mormon, to monitor his expedition's movements, and unannounced auto visits kept units alert.

Lt. George S. Patton, Jr., rich, arrogant, aggressive, used a Dodge touring car to lead a raid on a ranch, which led to the slaying of a ranking Villista captain. Not certain who had been killed, Patton lashed the corpse to a fender of his car and sought identification in a nearby village. He later wrote his wife: "You are probably wondering if my conscience hurts me for killing a man. It does not. I feel about it just as I did when I got my swordfish: surprised at my luck."[24] Patton's friend Major George T. Langhorne, used a chauffeur-driven Cadillac to chase Mexicans who had raided into Texas and then fled back across the border. Langhorne killed and captured several of the marauders, even though roads south of the Rio Grande were more of an adversary than the raiders.[25]

The use of vehicles expanded. Tractors replaced horses and mules to pull artillery; motor trucks equipped with radio sets accompanied advance columns; motorized ambulances jounced the sick and wounded mercilessly but got them to better hospitals; armored cars sent to bolster the spirits of citizens on the border were tested for war use; a wide variety of specialized support vehicles, such as rolling kitchens, kept the newly mobilized army fed, supplied, and in action. All this innovation paid off, as the Quartermaster Corps concluded in 1918, in the midst of World War I, "All the development of motor vehicles for military use in the United States Army has been the result of the Mexican punitive expedition. . . ."[26]

Land vehicles passed the test; the experience with a new air force was more spectacular, if less successful. With motor vehicles the army learned what worked; with airplanes, it learned what did not. When the First Aero Squadron was organized in early 1914 at San Diego, California, the U.S. ranked fourteenth in national air power, behind feudalistic Japan. Five pilots and thirty enlisted men assembled to fly three Martin T. biplanes. In the summer of 1915 the squadron moved to Fort Sill, Oklahoma, where it flew the new Curtiss JN-2—the famous Jenny—for artillery liaison work. In hopes of reducing the number of its military patrols monitoring the Mexican Revolution, the army moved the unit to the border in August 1915. Seven months later, eight dismantled planes, sent by train to Columbus, were reassembled and pronounced ready to serve the Pershing expedition.[27]

General Pershing ordered all eight aircraft to his headquarters outside Casas Grandes. They left

Columbus at 5:10 P.M. on March 19, confident that they could beat nightfall to their goal and avoid an unlighted, night landing. But serious miscalculations subverted their plan; slowed by winds, they scattered in the darkening night. Four landed safely at the pueblo of Ascensión. Three planes lost contact and drifted down where they could. Two of these made it; the third crashed, a total wreck. The eighth plane developed engine trouble soon after take-off and returned to Columbus. It was not an auspicious start for the army's first air squadron.[28]

The airmen enjoyed little improvement in the weeks that followed. The 95-horsepower engines of their Jennies counted only 4 horsepower above that necessary to fly at sea level. In the thinner air of Chihuahua's high plateau they barely cleared the pine tree tops, so there was no thought of negotiating the area's 10,000-foot mountains. Nor did they have sufficient power to handle the region's whirlwinds and terrifying vertical currents. By comparison, British, French, and German planes of the era could fly at 110 miles per hour and climb to 15,000 feet. Furthermore, European military commanders could call on their planes for a variety of services: reconnaissance and photomapping, air- to-ground wireless, artillery regulation, and bombardment. The U.S. Jennies were unarmed; pilots of the planes carried pistols. Two had high-powered .22 caliber rifles. Machine guns to arm new, improved planes and a supply of 100-pound bombs finally arrived at Columbus, but the aircraft never used them in Mexico.[29]

The airplanes managed some creditable photomapping with new automatic cameras; carried messages to "lost" columns; and when they managed to stay up long enough, conducted some reconnaissance. But they had one devil of a time staying up, and, if forced down, they became fair game for human scavengers. Mexicans marveled at the flying apparatuses, and missing parts of wrecked planes reappeared at their homesteads as adornments. When they literally pulled two planes apart at Chihuahua City, however, they were more angry than curious. The mob, abetted by Constitutionalist soldiers, burned cigarette holes in the wings, slashed the cloth sides with knives, and extracted nuts and bolts wherever their fingers could find them. The pilots took off for the relative safety of the outskirts of the city, and one made it. But a shower of stones tossed by the mob brought down the other, and the downed pilot held off his adversaries with a pistol until local authorities sent help.[30]

Miraculously, no pilots were killed or captured on any sortie in Mexico, truly miraculous because they frequently glided to crash landings in territory controlled by enemy Villistas, hostile Carrancistas, or unfriendly civilians. At times they used their sidearms to commandeer a horse or other assistance from a reluctant Mexican, but somehow, sooner or later, bruised and bloodied, often with broken bones, exhausted, half-starved, and dying of thirst, they made their way back to Pershing's headquarters or stumbled onto the path of an American scouting expedition. Their badly crippled planes were salvaged for parts (if they could beat the Mexicans to them) and then burned. It is difficult not to romanticize these fliers; they were brave, adventuresome, steadfast, and foolhardy. Despite their heroics, however, they could not keep their Jennies flying. The fault lay with the planes, not the men. Less than two months after first flying into Mexico, the army grounded the First Aero Squadron for good on the U.S. side of the border.[31]

If the infant air force disappointed military expectations in Mexico, experimentation with mobile kitchens and hospitals, with sanitation measures and medicines held promise. All soldiers received a variety of innoculations and bathed twice a week, under orders. The military also tried the new signal corps wireless equipment and tested improved weaponry, such as machine guns and artillery. Based on their Mexican experience, cavalry officers recommended numerous changes, from the size and breed of their horses to the types of canteens carried by the riders. Saddles, lariats, horseshoes, and rifles all received suggestions for improvements based on what had occurred in Mexico. Only the blankets carried by cavalrymen and their hats passed the test.[32]

Among the military challenges they faced, commanders up and down the line also struggled to deal with the problem of boredom among bivouacked troops; they responded with disciplined drills and tough training everyday. For relaxation, Pershing authorized a whorehouse called the "Remount Station" on his base (with Mexican girls, medically certified by U.S. doctors).

Records of the intelligence branch of the army reveal an imposing start for the Intelligence Service, as U.S. forces achieved a thorough penetration of Mexican communications, including coded messages. They seemed to know a good deal of Carranza's intentions; when he insisted that the Pershing expedition move in no direction but north—out of Mexico—he meant it.[33] President

Wilson expressed willingness to retire the expedition but still demanded guarantees and special considerations in return. Negotiations over these differences were interrupted periodically by clashes between contending troops in the field. Neither national leader could guarantee control of military commanders who were spoiling for a real fight and a series of sharp incidents again threatened to escalate into war.

Mexican raiders, eighty strong and perhaps including some Texans, in 1916 celebrated Cinco de Mayo by attacking two little settlements situated in the Texas Big Bend. At Glenn Springs, they killed three of the nine soldiers defending a wax factory and looted the local grocery store of all but its cans of sauerkraut and sacks of flour and corn too heavy to carry. At Boquillas, they emptied another store and kidnapped its owner and an employee. The U.S. military eagerly responded to the provocation. Two cavalry troops, one hundred men total, headed by dapper Major Langhorne in his eight-cylinder touring car, and followed by newsmen and motion picture cameramen in two Ford sedans, crossed into Mexico on May 11. "I'm clear of red tape," asserted Langhorne, "and I know of no Rio Grande."[34]

The "little Pershing expedition" lasted sixteen days. The very sight of it—at one point the Cadillac made nine miles in two hours—must have transfixed the Mexican robbers. How else could Langhorne have surprised them at their encampment? The troops killed several of the marauders and captured others. They recovered goods stolen from the two stores and rescued the two kidnapped men. Actually, the two had negotiated their own freedom before the soldiers arrived, but Langhorne claimed credit anyway. The entire nasty incident aroused little protest from the Mexican government but instigated a U.S. military policy of "hot pursuit." "Hot pursuit" signified limited invasion, but the limits were unspecified and elastic. Ignoring any diplomatic protocol, troops pursued into Mexico any Mexican bands that crossed the international line to raid United States territory, raising the possibility of war.[35]

Hot on the heels of Langhorne's venture and the inauguration of "hot pursuit" came the debacle for the United States at Carrizal. Carranza had formally warned Pershing not to move his command in any direction but north, or risk attack. Pershing, ordered to stay put by his own government, faced the shifting and concentration of Mexican forces which threatened the expedition. In June he learned that a large Mexican troop had camped at Villa Ahumada, seventy-five miles off his east flank, and ordered two troops of black cavalrymen under Captains Charles T. Boyd and Lewis S. Morley to investigate. He cautioned them to avoid any confrontation with the Mexican military.[36]

The little town of Carrizal, where some 400 Carrancista soldiers were stationed, lay between the Americans and their goal. As the troops approached the town, they were met by Mexican officers who denied them permission to pass through. Boyd could have gone around the town; he knew the Mexicans were dug in and had machine guns. After a series of fruitless meetings between the two parties, Captain Boyd exploded, "Tell the son-of-a-bitch [the Mexican commander] that I'm comin' through."[37] Pride, arrogance, and nationalism all overcame good judgment as Boyd ordered a dis-

mounted advance across 300 yards of open ground. The result was inevitable—a total defeat for the United States—and Boyd died with fourteen of his men. Ten wounded soldiers and twenty-five captured were taken to Chihuahua City. The Mexicans, even with forty-five killed and fifty-three wounded, could easily have captured everyone else, but they settled for the wounded and those who surrendered. American soldiers were humiliated on the battlefield and imprisoned by the enemy; now there had to be war. The army's chief of staff, Hugh Scott, expressed the consensus: "things look as if they are going to pop now."[38]

Carrizal lit the time bomb; the War Department alerted its field commanders. Pershing seemed to be particularly exposed to attack in Chihuahua; he had his men thinly stretched out along lines of communication, difficult to defend. Carranza could mass troops that would outnumber the Americans five to one. Washington believed that Pershing could successfully defend himself against an initial assault but would need reinforcements, especially if he were to take the offensive. With all this in mind and with the Americans captured at Carrizal, still the prisoners of the Constitutionalists, Wilson federalized the nation's entire state militia on June 18, 1916 and ordered the units to the border.[39]

The national emergency found most guard contingents at half strength and unprepared for active duty. It took the New York State militia, said to be the country's best, seven weeks to gear up. Not only men were needed, so were shoes, uniforms, and equipment. The field artillery and cavalry did not have enough horses—perhaps "enough to parade on Fifth Avenue," noted *Forum*, "but not enough to go to war."[40] The army's logistical system, little improved since its failures in the Indian Wars and notable disasters in the Spanish-American conflict, left many units short of rifles, machine guns, and ammunition, and weighted down with woolen "ODs" in which to face the desert heat. An Illinois regiment may have been the most fit of all the guard units for border duty; it had been playing war games for a motion picture company.[41]

Despite the shortcomings, recruitment for the militia soared as it never had for the regular army. No doubt, the army's seven-year enlistment deterred many young men. High wages in munitions plants and good farm prices also curtailed army recruitment, but in June 1916, school vacations and preparedness campaigns, such as that thundered by Roosevelt, created an enthusiasm for the militia. American youngsters, watching Europe, had grown curious about war, though to many, the Mexican venture could hardly be classified as war. One journalist called it "hunting big game."[42]

By midsummer, some 100,000 militiamen sweated out duty from San Diego, California, to Brownsville, Texas. They were not particularly skilled, officers no better than enlisted men. Less than 35 percent of the riflemen qualified as even second-class marksmen. In the contingent from Mississippi, only 7 of 1,467 riflemen qualified as expert. The army itself considered only 40 percent of the militiamen "efficient for battle purposes." Even when they were mustered out in late fall of 1916, 89 percent of the men ranked only fair to wholly unprepared for field service. The Militia Bureau of the War Department stated that it would take at least two years to train them up to acceptable standards, but their exaggerated calculations spoke to army requests for a larger appropriation from Congress.[43]

Fortunately for themselves and the country, soft and inexperienced militiamen never had to go to war against Mexico, although some were bloodied in border skirmishes. The eager young volunteers undoubtedly dreamed of storming south to the Halls of Montezuma, but they ended up sweltering in tents and on patrol in choking dust among prickly mesquite bushes. Their limited fighting experience included a mass fistfight, which broke out when the Michigan band tramped through the Georgia tent area playing "Marching through Georgia."[44]

On duty they built sandbag fortifications and pontoon bridges, dug ditches and repaired rails, engaged in tactical training manuevers, and experimented with newfangled equipment. Off duty, they explored a region new to most of them. They adopted as mascots local creatures with which they were not familiar, such as rattlesnakes and gila monsters. For recreation they shot craps, tossed each other in blankets, and visited the "working girls" south of El Paso's Eighth Street, or that city's Mexican quarter, Chihuahuita, with its open-air stands and limited sanitary conditions. Lots of the men suffered stomach disorders (nothing serious, only diarrhea); occasionally one got into trouble, shot somebody, and deserted.[45] Civilian reformers clamored for military canteens to keep the young men out of "these hellholes."[46] So the army created canteens, serving only 2.5 percent beer, which John Dos Passos labeled the "first fruits of twenty years of agitation for prohibition."[47] Despite the efforts of the concerned citizens, the "hellholes" did not dry up.

The tour on the border offered sunburn, heat prostration, cracked lips, blistered feet, and occasionally venereal disease. Mexican raiders killed a few guardsmen at isolated outposts, and others died in training accidents. While their overall efficiency ratings may not have been the highest, the men learned to endure and to soldier. Sixty-five of the ninety-two cavalrymen on border duty from Lynchburg, Virginia, served as officers in World War I.[48] Officers assigned to the border began to see that pomp and circumstance were less important than good logistics, a lesson that proved important later on, in combat elsewhere.

Although President Wilson may not have realized—or could not publicly admit—that the border experience provided vitally important training for Europe's wars, many of the soldiers knew it. So did the postcard manufacturers who printed the message on their cards: "Our infantry had a taste of genuine trench-digging [true] and trench-fighting [not true] while guarding the Texas border last summer. . . . Anyway, the time they spent down there and the things they learned will prove invaluable to them when they get over to France and get after the Kaiser's men." And on the back of a card showing a pontoon bridge built over the Rio Grande: "[This] is another example of an obstacle overcome by well-known American pluck and Yankee ingenuity. Our troops across the sea will give a good account of themselves in thousands of clever, practical ways just as surely as they will by their bravery in battle."[49]

The mobilization certainly provided for an unforeseen and unparalleled market for picture post-cards. Thousands of mass-produced postcards offer a lucid, all-too-human record of daily life on duty (and off) along the border. Although at times the pictures belie their words, the men who bought and sent the cards tell us what they thought of their experience, or at least what they wanted others to believe about it.

•

Reflect upon some of the thousands of picture postcards made of military life along the border, a selection of which is displayed at the end of this chapter. The spirited enthusiasm that the national guardsmen brought with them to the border was quickly eroded by routine. You can see the boredom in their eyes and in their demeanor on the photo postcards.[50] Although the food supposedly was quite good, especially on Sundays, the boys pictured on chow lines look sullen. One soldier wrote that he had guard duty at the cookhouse. "It's not to keep the Mexicans out as much as our own boys. You know that I will fill up in the morning." Nevertheless there are few smiles, even among the men seated for a traditional Thanksgiving dinner. Food was not enough; they lacked military action and wanted to be home. The Massachusetts guard raised a banner: "We want to fight or go home."[51]

Soldiers from Grand Rapids, Michigan, posed for a special-edition picture postcard; on the front they noted that they were on the border, far from home on a traditional holiday: "I wonder if you think of me, on this Thanksgiving Day." A lined, white space followed, for the sender to fill in his name. For Christmas, "Holiday Greetings from the Mexican Border. When Christmas bells ring out, these tho'ts we're feeling: We're lonesome here, down on the Rio Grande; So here's a Merry Christmas from the Border, Where the Boys are all a mighty lonesome band."

By Thanksgiving 1916 a lot of guardsmen were asking why they were still there. One group posed with pitchforks instead of rifles, another with a shovel. The soldier from Mineral Wells, Texas, who drew cartoons on the front of his postcards, pictured himself behind bars at a jailhouse window shaped like an official government badge, stars at the top; the stripes were his bars. "On the inside looking out," read the inscription. His months of army service at Big Bend weighed heavily. On another card he drew soldiers with supplies riding a wagon up to its hubs in south Texas sand. A trooper questions, "Is this Big Bend country?" Comes the reply: "They should turn it into a National Park for Indians, wild animals and tourists."[52]

The militiamen could gripe with the best; their cards are filled with minor peeves. A poem of complaints by bugler James J. Verhoeks, 32nd Michigan Infantry, became an oversized postcard:

> I've done my bit on the border
> > I wish I was in God's country again
> I've had my fill of the border
> > Of Greasers and Border men
> I've eaten the dirt of Texas
> > I've drank of the Rio Grande
> I've grubbed mesquite in the cursed heat
> > (The Lord never made the land)
>
> . . .
>
> I've dug in the blasted trenches
> > The air was a hundred hells—
> I've charged in the jungle cactus
> > To the music of rebel yells.

Verhoeks was proud that "I've followed the flag of my country," and he concluded that, "I wouldn't trade the friends I've made, For all I've lost in [the] game."[53] Still, he had had his fill of the border and wanted to go home. So did many of his buddies who had indeed lost a good deal in the "game." Some of them had sacrificed substantial salaries needed to support their families. Others left behind small businesses which suffered in their absence.

Off-duty fun and recreation placated the disgruntled soldiers. To the people back home, they were guarding their morals as well as the border. No photo postcards showed visits to the raucous and raunchy Mexican quarter of El Paso. Instead they portrayed plenty of traditional wholesome play: tug-of-war, blanket tossings, polo, boxing, and basketball, all reinforced by masses of men posing with a priest in front of the recreation center of the Knights of Columbus, or attending outdoor church services, or posed before the Young Men's Christian Association Hall. The YMCA even put out its own postcard:

This is part of the World-Wide movement conducted by the International Committee of the Young Men's Christian Association, in cooperation with the various state committees and local associations, made possible by the generosity of friends throughout the country. Each building serves about 3,000 men. Daily facts: average attendance, 2,000. Stationery used, 2,000 sheets. Stamps sold, $40.00. Games played, 500. Building filled to capacity each night at religious services, entertainments and concerts.

The YMCA proudly did its share of social control.[54]

However, the propagandistic postcards of the YMCA did not seem to appeal to the troops; the men preferred those cards which insinuated superiority over an enemy that they never had fought. Harold showed his mother a huge mass of charred corpses with the message: "Burning the dead after an engagement." To complement the picture of an executed Mexican soldier, a trooper wrote, "Thought I'd send a little word from Matamoros. How do you like this? See where they went through the dead's pockets." And on the back of a photo of a teenage boy, "This boy fought all day and night in the trenches and was captured and shot with 15 others the following morning." Occasionally, a Mexican received a faint tribute; on a picture of Pascual Orozco, "This is the Gick that knows how to fight." More often the messages approximated that on a photo of General Maytorena: "He murdered people in wholesale lots down here. Does he look like it?" It did not seem to matter who wrote the postcards, from what town, during what period; from the sailors and marines at Veracruz to the infantrymen and cavalry troops all along the border, U.S. military personnel saw Mexican rebels as bandits and greasers, better dead than alive.

If border duty was long on experience, it was short on pay. The guardsmen earned about $15 a month, so money and money deals were on their minds. "We got paid the 21st and I am broke today the 22nd," a soldier wrote to his parents, "but we have a canteen here in camp that you can get anything with checks. You are allowed 4 dollars worth of checks a month." Archie Hutchinson thought his brother, Donald, in Kingston, Pennsylvania, might be interested in buying a horse: "You can buy a good horse down here for $50. One fellow in our battery bought one for $35, 3½ years old and

about 14 hands high. He was too small for army regulations but sure is a bargain."

Money may have tempted more than one soldier to desert. Mexican commanders needed skilled personnel to operate new weapons and vehicles which had suddenly become available through foreign imports. Dynamiters were sought to blow rail lines and other communications. Promises of high pay made it worth the risk for some; others simply craved combat; a few had personal problems. Whatever their motivation, Americans more than occasionally deserted their units to serve the Mexicans; postcard senders wrote about it: "This is a picture of a machinegun, a trained operator can fire 420 shots a minute with one of these. When an American soldier deserts and goes over to Mexico and handles one there, they usually pay him from $6 to $10 a day. I mean $6 to $10 in Mexican money which is about 30 cents in real, human money." The writer concluded with a thought that probably gave potential deserters some pause: "As a rule they shoot a man the day before payday. Payday occurs about once a year." Whether the statement reflected reality or rumor is unclear.

Most of the men seldom thought of desertion and, in general, were proud of serving their country; most of all, the troops just wanted to go home. They requested more hometown newspapers to pass around among their buddies from the same place, and they wanted not to be forgotten. One asked that his postcards be posted in the local store back home along with a typed copy of the message on the other side. Personal, and at times quite poignant, messages frequently appeared on the postcards. The soldiers increasingly missed their friends and family. They worried about their wives and wondered if their children were doing well in school. Border life had its moments, as when a bobcat crawled into a soldier's tent at night, or when a sandstorm blew down half a camp, or when a flash flood reached the level of the cots in their tents. In the main, the men quickly tired of, as they said it, "waging peace on the Mexican border."[55]

•

The mobilized guard did not go to war in Mexico because Venustiano Carranza had nothing to gain by provoking such a conflict, and Woodrow Wilson resisted considerable pressure. The U.S. Army urged Wilson to permit an aggressive campaign against Pancho Villa. Some wanted to push on even further, but the president, fearing another Carrizal, not to mention war with Mexico, refused. One of Pershing's cavalry commanders later reflected, "War with Mexico in the spring of 1916 would have been a splendid preliminary to our entrance in the World War. Half a million men would have cleaned up Mexico in quick order."[56]

Carranza released the American prisoners captured at Carrizal before they had become a cause célèbre for full-scale intervention, and his decision allowed the United States to relax its warlike stance and to return to negotiations. The Americans agreed to start withdrawing the Pershing expedition once the Constitutionalists proved they had the will, determination, and means to eradicate Villismo and to maintain domestic order. Carranza assured Wilson that public peace was being achieved (although it was not, and both sides knew it). He insisted—and this remained the major stumbling block—that the Pershing mission leave Mexico

forthwith, without time schedule or delay. He even encouraged incursions into south Texas to impress the Wilson administration with the strength of his arguments. The forays were similar to, but not as extensive as, those Carranza had fostered in relation to the now defunct Plan of San Diego.

By late 1916 Villa had made a strong (but even today, poorly understood) comeback. The revolution in Chihuahua, it seems, had not run its course; substantial numbers of people for myriad reasons favored Villa over Carranza, or thought differences could only be settled on the battlefield. Villa's army captured the state capital of Chihuahua, abandoned it, and then reoccupied it before being driven off once again. The first time in town he freed prisoners from the state penitentiary, and in a speech from the balcony of the Governor's Palace, he promised people liberty. The Carrancista soldiers not only could not contain Villa, but they often deserted to his cause, ambiguous as it was. Federal commanders did not aggressively pursue him, apparently responding to local political maneuvering, perhaps linked to national affairs.[57]

Carranza himself was busy with other things; he called a convention to rewrite the nation's constitution, and the new version promulgated on February 1, 1917 was more liberal than either he or Woodrow Wilson (and American business interests in Mexico) would have liked.[58]

Wilson too had other concerns. Germany had reinaugurated unrestricted submarine warfare, and Wilson was about to ask Congress for a declaration of war. Problems with Mexico, still troublesome, had to be resolved. War with Germany mandated peace with Mexico. So Wilson granted Carranza's long-time demands: negotiations toward *de jure* diplomatic recognition and withdrawal of the Pershing expedition. With the president's critics yelling "unconditional surrender," the last of Pershing's troops exited Mexico with little public notice on February 5, 1917. Events in Europe eclipsed the withdrawal, and the nation's press headlined the coming war with Germany. The national guardsmen who gradually had been mustered out of service returned to their home states to await recruitment for the "real war."[39]

With their principal market gone and their subject matter overshadowed, the picture postcard producers along the border closed up shop. It had been an exciting, at times zany, often laborious, and reasonably profitable six or seven years. The photographers probably never thought that their cards would be the subject of a book, or that hobbyists would compete, at times frantically and even deviously, and pay extraordinary prices for samples of their work. But here you have them, picture postcards, a marvelously human and highly valuable record of our past.

The results of Watchful Waiting
Columbus

In the aftermath of the Columbus raid, criticism of President Wilson's policy of "watchful waiting" toward Mexico appeared on photo postcards—one of the few times during the period that postcards carried a political message. (Courtesy John Hardman Collection.)

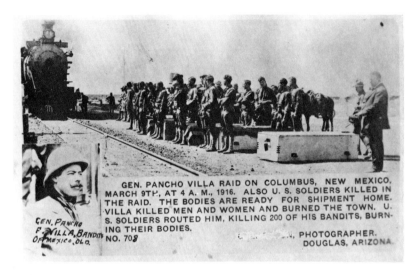

GEN. PANCHO VILLA RAID ON COLUMBUS, NEW MEXICO,
MARCH 9TH, AT 4 A. M., 1916. ALSO U. S. SOLDIERS KILLED IN
THE RAID. THE BODIES ARE READY FOR SHIPMENT HOME.
VILLA KILLED MEN AND WOMEN AND BURNED THE TOWN. U.
S. SOLDIERS ROUTED HIM, KILLING 200 OF HIS BANDITS, BURN-
ING THEIR BODIES.
GEN. PANCHO
F. VILLA, BANDIT NO. 708
OF MEXICO, OLD.
........., PHOTOGRAPHER.
DOUGLAS, ARIZONA

One version of the Columbus attack, calculated to sell postcards to Americans: Villa and his murderous bandits versus heroic and avenging U.S.
soldiers. (Courtesy John Hardman Collection.)

Wounded Mexicans, not particularly well attended, were a curiosity to American troopers, who never tired of posing with their victims. (Courtesy El Paso Public Library.)

These twelve Mexican prisoners were tried for complicity in the raid on Columbus. Ten were convicted; of those, seven were executed and three imprisoned. The other two men were exonerated and freed. (Courtesy Carter Rila Collection.)

An eyewitness to the battle recounted: "The real horror lay in the streets and on the sidewalks. Villa's men who had fallen lay dead and dying. Some twitched, some mumbled, most were sprawled in the abandoned posture of death. Except for an occasional curse, they were left ignored. Later in the day they were gathered, stacked and burned." (Courtesy Carter Rila Collection.)

Dead Bandits being Identified at Columbus N.M.

A body count in Mexico followed the raid. Villa's rear guard resolutely resisted—and paid the price—so that their commander and the main body of his cavalry could escape southward into the friendly Valley of Papigochic. (Courtesy John Hardman Collection.)

Despite local fears that Villa might return to Columbus, he did not. Instead, within a week the U.S. Army under General Pershing had taken charge. A resident remembers: "Grown-up talk centered around catching and punishing Pancho Villa. In our childish minds, he became villain, ogre, and arch enemy. Our games changed to 'Soldiers chasing Bandits,' and we galloped through the brush and peered stealthily around adobe corners." (Courtesy Carter Rila Collection.)

Truck Train in Mexico

KAVANAUGH'S WAR POSTALS

"And then the day arrived when General Pershing planned to enter Mexico!
Men, horses, field artillery, trucks, supplies, repair units, all poised for the start.
As usual, the townspeople were caught up in the great moment—at last—retri-
bution was at hand. It would be the culminating show." (Courtesy John
Hardman Collection.)

The soldiers shouldered a nine-pound Springfield rifle and carried bandoliers
of ammunition in five-round clips. A bayonet, first aid pouch, canteen, and
machete hung from their web belts. Among things in their packs were a
poncho, blanket, mess kit, can of bacon, a couple of pairs of socks and under-
shorts, a towel and toothbrush, rifle-cleaning gear, a "housewife" (needle,
thread, and buttons), and maybe some dice, playing cards, condoms, roll-
your-own tobacco, a pencil—and yes, some postcards. (Courtesy John
Hardman Collection.)

U.S. Soldiers Resting under Shade Trees at Colonia Diaz.

Mexicans, soldiers as well as civilians, intensely loathed Pershing's expedition (they considered it an invasion). To lessen tension the Americans set up headquarters at a largely evacuated Mormon colony at Casas Grandes, Chihuahua. As the campaign bogged down in high-level diplomatic negotiations, the site became a military training camp with the usual maneuvers, drills, diversions, and hangers-on. The Chihuahua summer burned and irritated their unprotected faces, so the soldiers stopped shaving and grew beards. An observer commented that the soldiers resembled Old Testament characters and addressed each other by biblical names. (Courtesy El Paso Public Library.)

'IN COLONIA DUBLAN.
MEXICO

Pershing permitted an official whorehouse, called the "remount station," on the base. The girls, inspected and certified "safe" by military doctors, were Mexicans from Ciudad Juárez, the madam a Mexican-American from El Paso. Criticism from U.S. moralists went unanswered. The photographer who turned this picture into a postcard averred that the women shown were prostitutes at Pershing's camp. But there is room for doubt. In appearance, these women do not seem to be prostitutes, but an enterprising photographer would not have hesitated to label them so, had he thought it might increase the sales of his cards. (Courtesy Carter Rila Collection.)

Chinese refugees fled to the safety of the fringes of the U.S. camp and soon established themselves as petty merchants in makeshift huts. Marauding Mexican armies looted their properties and mercilessly persecuted, even murdered, them throughout northern Mexico. (Courtesy El Paso Public Library.)

Shops, restaurants, and laundries, their prices controlled by the army's Chinese-American provost marshal, soon dotted the entire route from Columbus to Pershing's headquarters. When the expedition left Mexico, the Chinese went north with it. Despite the legal infraction (the Chinese exclusion law was still in effect), immigration authorities permitted them to stay as long as the military guaranteed that the Chinese would not become a public charge. They did not, because the army put them to work as cooks and in other utility tasks that the average soldier was only too glad to shun. (Courtesy Carter Rila Collection.)

U.S. Cavalry awaiting arrival of Bodies of the Victims
of the Battle of Carrizal, Mex.

With the defeat of the American contingents at Carrizal on June 21, 1916 and the capture of twenty-three U.S. troopers who were imprisoned in Chihuahua City, the U.S. and Mexico were poised for all-out war. Carranza, however, chose not to risk it. He released the captives and sent them by train to the border where U.S. cavalry units, an army chaplain, and most of El Paso waited to greet them as returning heroes. (Courtesy Carter Rila Collection.)

The returnees from Carrizal, nationally as famous as any American warriors had ever been, hardly looked the part as they trudged across the International Bridge at El Paso. They had been stripped of their uniforms. One wore a blanket, a few were barefoot, others wore huaraches (Mexican sandals). The men were escorted to a delousing station and reissued military dress. (Courtesy Carter Rila Collection.)

Bodies of the Victims of the Battle of Carrizal, Mex. being returned to El Paso, Tex.

An even more somber sight for the thousands who lined El Paso's streets was the return of the bodies of American servicemen, among the twelve killed at Carrizal. (Courtesy Carter Rila Collection.)

El Paso Tex Jule 14/916
JtBenn

Cavalrymen who were captured at the
Battle of Carrizal. Released by Mexico

Holding bouquets of flowers given them by sympathetic crowds, the ex-prisoner members of the Black Troops "C" and "K" of the 10th U.S. Calvary, posed for this group photo which became a famous postcard. In the center, wearing the white yachting cap which was his trademark, is Lemuel Spillsburg, a Mormon scout who accompanied the ill-fated expedition to Carrizal and who advised the commander in charge to avoid the conflict by marching around the town. The commander, Captain Charles T. Boyd, was spoiling for a fight, and it cost him his life. (Courtesy John Hardman Collection.)

The president's call to mobilize the national guard found the state militia units in dismal degrees of unpreparedness. The best-trained and equipped unit among them may have been from Illinois, where it was involved in making a movie. (Courtesy John Hardman Collection.)

RECRUITS FOR MEXICAN SERVICE JUST ARRIVED (20)

The Kansas National Guard resembled early pioneers as it rolled through Austin, Texas, in covered wagons en route to the Mexican border. The men were soon thrust into the ambiance of modern military training. (Courtesy Kansas State Historical Society.)

Volunteer Truck ready for run to any threatening point on the Border, this Truck first Volunteer Truck made overland test trip from Chicago (2100 Miles) in Fourteen days

Plenty of bombast accompanied the journey to the international line. (Courtesy El Paso Public Library.)

New recruits rapidly filled the depleted ranks of the state guards; the overall response by the nation's young men to "Get Villa" was overwhelming, although some—including this cartoonist—hinted at reservations. (Courtesy John Hardman Collection.)

The militiamen came to fight, to storm the Halls of Montezuma in Mexico City, as their American predecessors had done. Instead, the troops "watched and waited" in accordance with national policy. They also learned to dig trenches for warfare and practiced deployment in them—lessons which later proved useful in France. (Courtesy John Hardman Collection.)

Sand Storm in Camp.

W. H. Horne Co
El Paso, Tex.

They also battled the infamous Texas sand devils, along with flash floods and temperatures well above 100°. During dust storms men inside the tents wore goggles, had bandanas over their mouths, lay on their stomachs, and hoped that stones used to weigh down the tents held in place. (Courtesy Carter Rila Collection.)

During the mobilization the frequent military parades in El Paso impressed the Mexicans with the burgeoning U.S. presence and assured Anglo residents of the city that they would be protected against Pancho Villa, as well as any disturbances by the city's Mexican population, which detested Pershing's intervention. (In 1916 the population of El Paso was 52 percent Mexican or Mexican-American; in addition, the city housed thousands of refugees.) (Courtesy El Paso Public Library.)

Numbers of Americans, military and otherwise, believed that the way to catch Pancho Villa was with a motor car, which proves how little they knew of the man's tactics and fortitude, not to speak of the terrain and public sentiment in Chihuahua. (Courtesy John Hardman Collection.)

Knights of Columbus halls and YMCAs erected at military posts along the border provided light entertainment and guarded the morals of the boys. At the end of its six-month stint along the international line, the YMCA announced that it had served the troops "in a most striking way:"

Estimated attendance	7,871,468
Estimated number of letters written (free stationery furnished)	5,059,274
Estimated attendance at entertainments	2,851,316
Estimated attendance at lectures	105,494
Estimated attendance at religious meetings	681,407
Bible classes	13,663
Forward step decisions	20,012
Joined Enlisted Men's Bible and Prayer League	14,154
Decisions for Christian Life	13,845
Renewal of Christian purpose	2,242
Personal interviews	22,375
Scriptures distributed	45,470
Visits to sick	67,680
Pieces of reading matter distributed	398,921

(Courtesy Carter Rila Collection.)

The men even drew cartoonlike postcards to show how army service had shaped them up. (Courtesy John Hardman Collection.)

The soldiers also posed for photos which showed them on the ready alert. They wanted to assure people back home that they were ready for action, even though they understood that no such military activity was ever likely to occur. (Courtesy Carter Rila Collection.)

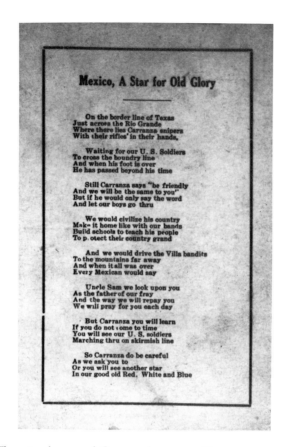

They sternly warned Carranza in poetry: Come to terms with
Uncle Sam or face an invasion and occupation. (Courtesy
John Hardman Collection.)

S.D. 87½

And they developed some war stories. A soldier wrote on the back of this card: "These are different types of guns and revolvers captured from native bandits lately. They are rather antique but Uncle Sam decided they were to [sic] dangerous for them to have. They might go off accidentally, you know, and kill a marine." (Courtesy Andreas Brown Collection.)

Despite their boasts, the militiamen were bored stiff, increasingly so as time wore on. They said it in a variety of ways, but few more pointedly than in the postcards that Joseph "Jodie" Pickens Harris, III, drew at his isolated post in Texas Big Bend country. Harris sent them home to Mineral Wells, Texas, to be displayed in the local drugstore. (Courtesy Special Collections, Sul Ross State University Library.)

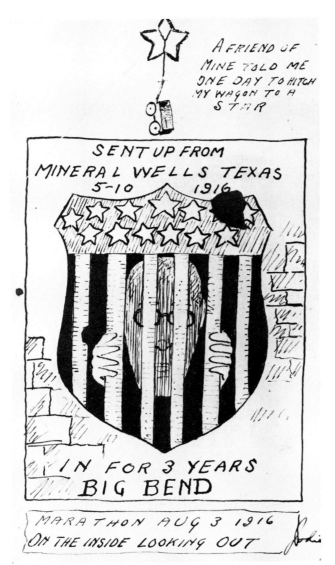

Harris equated military duty with a prison sentence. (Courtesy Special Collections, Sul Ross State University Library.)

Jodie Harris could be blatantly political, and his cards give evidence about aspects of border strife which professional historians have yet to investigate. For instance, on this postcard Americans are accused of deliberately instigating banditry in their own border territory in order to frustrate peace negotiations then under way. (Courtesy Special Collections, Sul Ross State University Library.)

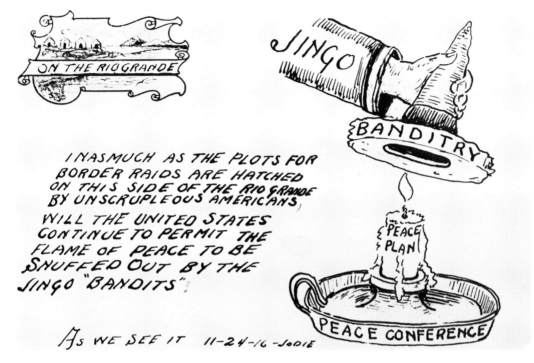

ON THE RIO GRANDE

INASMUCH AS THE PLOTS FOR
BORDER RAIDS ARE HATCHED
ON THIS SIDE OF THE RIO GRANDE
BY UNSCRUPLEOUS AMERICANS,

WILL THE UNITED STATES
CONTINUE TO PERMIT THE
FLAME OF PEACE TO BE
SNUFFED OUT BY THE
JINGO "BANDITS"?

AS WE SEE IT 11-24-16 -JODIE

JINGO
BANDITRY
PEACE PLAN
PEACE CONFERENCE

In another broadside Harris charges U.S. moneyed interests with fomenting disorder along the border in order to provoke a military invasion of Mexico—the inference being to protect and to further their Mexican business interests. So sharp were Harris' barbs that they raise the question of the whereabouts of military censorship. Certainly it existed. Perhaps the censors never saw the Harris cards, which only travelled the relatively remote route from the Big Bend to Mineral Wells, Texas. If they had, they probably would have acted. The role and limits of military censorship was another policy and practical consideration being tested, largely for the first time, during the troubles along the border. (Courtesy Special Collections, Sul Ross State University Library.)

I'VE DONE MY BIT ON THE BORDER

(By Bugler JAMES J. VERHOEKS,
Co. F, 32nd Michigan Inf.)

I've done my bit on the border
    I wish I was in God's country again
I've had my fill of the border
    Of Greasers and border men
I've eaten the dirt of Texas
    I've drank of the Rio Grande
I've grubbed mesquite in the cursed heat
    (The Lord never made the land)
I've seen all there is on the border
    I've felt all there is to feel
I've done my time in a sea of slime
I've lost all they didn't steal.

I've carried a pack in a jungle
    Till it cut me down to the blood
I've sweltered and lay like a thing of clay
    In a slithering swamp of mud
I've risen at five in the morning
    At the sound of a reville
I've slaved all day for newsboy's pay
    Till the night would set me free
I've lived the life of a soldier
    No chance to "beat it " or shirk
And the life of a soldier, believe me,
Is little but damned hard work.

I've done my bit on the border
    At El Paso and the Mesa sands
I've hiked and sweat in the heat and wet
From Las Cruces to the end of the land
I've done the camps at Cotton
    At Stewart and Pershing
I've lain in the dust and gnawed a crust
    At Bell's judgment seat
I've eaten meals with reptiles
    I've quartered with bugs galore
In a land where things are all made with strings
From the trees to the rugs on the floor
I've dug in the blasted trenches
    The air was a hundred hells—
I've charged in the jungle cactus
    To the music of rebel yells.

I've eaten the food of a soldier
    Hardtack and Mulligan stew
Bacon and beans, and a touch of greens
    But Lord, they were scarce and few.
I've followed the flag of my country
    In kahki and plain O. D.
And up to date I am standing straight
    In a way that is good to see
I've done my bit on the border
    I've had my fill of the same
But I wouldn't trade the friends I've made
    For all I've lost in the game.

A poem, reproduced on thousands of postcards, summed up the sentiments of a good many troopers: they had done their duty on the border, such as it was, and now they wanted to go home. (Courtesy Andreas Brown Collection.)

The army tried to salve the growing discontent among the militiamen by serving a special meal on a traditional holiday, Thanksgiving 1916. (Courtesy Carter Rila Collection.)

The troops were not easily placated, and they showed it in their group photos. Whereas they once had proudly posed with their rifles and other sorts of modern military equipment, symbols of discontent began to appear: in this case a shovel—to shovel the . . . . (Courtesy Carter Rila Collection.)

And here with pitchforks, perhaps for the same purpose. (Courtesy Carter Rila Collection.)

35 Motor Trucks delivering Supplies to U.S. Army in Mexico.

W. H. Horne Co.
El Paso, Tex.

Reasons why the U.S. Army straddled the Mexican border for such a long period of time are still being debated, but one result is clear: time on the frontier gave the military an opportunity to modernize and to test new equipment, logistical procedures, field operations, intelligence gathering, in short, to bring America's army into the twentieth century. One of the most striking and controversial aspects of this process concerned the motorization of the military—at the expense of the time-worn and highly romanticized cavalry. As it turned out, both had their uses in Mexico, but ostentatious truck displays like this one were meant to warn Mexico of America's new might and tell the rest of the world of this nation's coming of military age. The U.S. Army first used four-wheel-drive vheicles on the border during this epoch. Among them were the famous Jeffrey Quads out of Kenosha, Wisconsin, and three-ton, four-by-four cargo (FWD^s), springless and with wooden tires from Clintonville, Wisconsin. (Courtesy Carter Rila Collection.)

There were no roads, paved or otherwise, in the regions of Chihuahua where the expedition was chasing Pancho Villa, only wagon trails with high centers. The trucks had to forge their own paths; they soon dug great furrows in soft, alkali soil of the sector, which in the rainy season became a quagmire into which the trucks sank up to their hubcaps. A good many trucks became so mired in the muck that they had to be stripped of their parts and abandoned to the elements and human scavengers. (Courtesy Andreas Brown Collection.)

Sample of Military Roads on the Border and in Mexico

Pershing's demand for trucks created a scramble among manufacturers anxious to secure military contracts. The result meant no standardization among the types of vehicles. In all, thirteen different types came from eight different manufacturers. Most common were one-half-ton, 4×2 trucks. The record speed for the 104-mile truck trip between Columbus and Pershing's headquarters at the Mormon colony was ten hours. Some ran up to 15 miles per hour for short stretches over smooth terrain. As seen in this photo, under circumstances all too common to the area, horses often had much the better going than did motor vehicles. (Courtesy Carter Rila Collection.)

Soldiers assigned to the truck companies posed for photographs with the civilian truck drivers, but they did not like each other. The civilians, needed because the army had no trained drivers of its own, made five times the monthly pay of an ordinary soldier and experienced less military regimen. (Courtesy Carter Rila Collection.)

Motorcycles, despite their maneuverability, lived one of the shortest lives in the army's experimentation with motorized vehicles. Jarring chuckholes and rocky ravines south of the border quickly relegated the cycles, mostly Harley-Davidsons and Hendees (Indians), to communications work on the few graded and paved roads which existed near the major camps on the U.S. side. (Courtesy Andreas Brown Collection.)

Gunners could get no concentrated fire from weapons mounted on the armored sidecars attached to the motorcycles. As they bounced along, they wildly and ineffectively sprayed the countryside with bullets. Stray cattle suffered the result. (Courtesy Murney Gurlach Collection.)

First Armored Motor Battery in Action.

Socially prominent and wealthy "warriors" manned many of the national guard units, and any number brought their state-of-the-art touring cars, thoroughbred horses, and personally approved weapons with them to the border. No guard unit was more elitist than that of New York; following Villa's "insult" to national pride, the well-to-do and jingoistic New Yorkers were spoiling for a fight and eagerly financed the creation of the First Armored Motor Battery of the N.Y. National Guard. Its equipment included seventy-two motorcycles, two trucks, and a staff car, as well as three armored cars. In a flurry of experimentation with armor, vehicle manufacturers assembled boiler plates in a variety of designs over their respective truck chassis and shipped their creations to the border. This Mack armored car, constructed by the International Motor Company of New York, had Colt machine guns mounted on barbettes that could pivot and swing. B. T. White describes it in *Tanks and Other Armored Fight Vehicles, 1900 to 1918:*

[It] had a straightforward open top armored hull, somewhat better in design than many of its contemporaries in that the top half was sloped inwards to improve its ballistic properties. Two Colt machine-guns with curved shields were mounted staggered in the rear part where they had a good field of fire. The engine air intake at the front was protected by adjustable shutters. [Its modified cooling system had an oversized radiator.] The chassis was basically that of the Mack 2-ton, 144-in. wheelbase truck, with worn drive and dual rear wheels while the tyres were formed of solid rubber blocks. A big vehicle [its armor alone weighed 3,000 pounds] the Mack armoured car was 19 ft. 8 in. long, 6 ft. 6 in. wide, and 8 ft. 4 in. high (to top of gun shields) and weighed 4½ (short) tons. (Courtesy John Hardman Collection.)

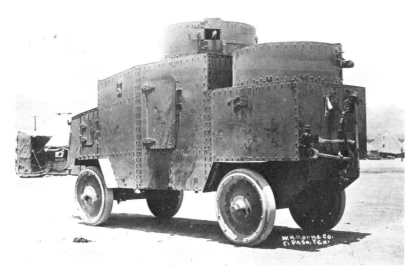

This Jeffrey Quad (four-wheel drive) was noted for its ruggedness, and the British had used it in India before the U.S. tested improvements along the border. It carried two machine guns and a six-man crew and was powered by a four-cylinder Buda engine that developed nearly forty horsepower. Side armor plating was one-half-inch thick. (Courtesy John Hardman Collection.)

Armored motor car for attacking aeroplanes

Although the Mexicans had no air force, American soldiers-of-fortune and mercenaries flew U.S.-made planes for the Villistas and Carrancistas, depending upon which side paid the most. Antiaircraft armored cars never saw action against these planes, but they remained part of the general motorized build-up being tested along the international line—if not for combat in Mexico, then for a forthcoming struggle in Europe, which many suspected was drawing near. This 1916 White armored car carried a .30 caliber Benet-Mercier machine gun in its turret and a crew of three men. Its 36-horsepower engine could drive it up to forty miles per hour. Its armor was only a quarter-of-an-inch thick, but the vehicle weighed almost 7,500 pounds. (Courtesy John Hardman Collection.)

U.S. Army Airplane arriving at a Villiage in Mexico.

The First Aero Squadron flew eight of these JN-3s ("Jennies") in support of the Pershing expedition. These biplanes were the best manufactured at the time and were even strengthened for border service. But Mexican conditions defeated the planes: their wheels sank in the sand so that they could not gather sufficient air speed to take off; gusty winds and sudden down drafts buffeted the machines; low humidity dried out the wooden propellers so that the laminations began to separate; the 90-to-100 horsepower engines did not provide sufficient lift to allow them to clear the Sierra Madre. After scarcely more than one month's service, only two "Jennies" remained in commission, and these were deemed unsafe for further flights. They were flown back to Columbus, condemned, and destroyed. (Courtesy Andreas Brown Collection.)

Ready to Leave the Ground, El Paso, Texas

Take-off on a harrowing reconnaissance mission, the pilot seated in the rear, his observer up front. The planes were unarmed; they carried no bombs, although most of the pilots had a pistol for personal protection after a nearly inevitable forced landing in hostile territory. (Courtesy Carter Rila Collection.)

Despite the shortcomings of their aircraft—still highly experimental and the subject of constant modification—the pilots displayed great verve and perseverance, among them Ira A. Rader, J. E. Carberry, Carlton G. Chapman, Townsend F. Dodd, E. S. Gorrell, H. A. Dargue, A. R. Christie, and W. G. Kilner. For a month they flew almost daily reconnaissance flights, tested new aerial photography equipment, and tightened communications between the operation ground units and their headquarters. They also testified before (and complained to) government investigating agencies about the deficiencies of their planes and demanded improvements which helped to usher America into the air age. (Courtesy Carter Rila Collection.)

Military Observation Balloon

Balloons were the eyes of the army artillery, and the mobilization gave units the opportunity to experiment with the new Kite balloons—nicknamed sausages—which proved to have more lift and stability than former spherical balloons. Filled with helium, these "captive" balloons were anchored to a windlass some two to five miles behind imaginary battlelines, but never saw combat along the border. A national guard unit tested this balloon, gift of the Goodyear Tire and Rubber Company of Akron, Ohio, and lessons learned soon proved valuable in France. (Courtesy Andreas Brown Collection.)

The Caquot captive observation balloon could carry two observers up some 5,000 feet. It was ninty-three feet long, twenty-eight feet in diameter, held 37,500 cubic feet of gas, and was considered the class of its day. Successful test flights during the mobilization encouraged its use in World War I, where enemy fire limited its average longevity to fifteen days. Once the bag was hit and the gas began to burn, the observers had fifteen to twenty seconds to bail out before the balloon exploded. (Courtesy Carter Rila Collection.)

The U.S. military intelligence service was, in effect, founded during the epoch of the Pershing expedition. The most sophisticated eavesdropping equipment available tapped into Mexican communications lines and furnished detailed information about troop movements and political intentions to Pershing and to Washington, D.C. Unaware of this new U.S. capability, the Mexicans did not bother to encode many of their messages, laying bare their plans to their adversary. (Courtesy Andreas Brown Collection.)

FIELD WIRELESS.

At the tactical level in Chihuahua, public resentment at the American invasion made U.S. field communications difficult. Civilians cut telephone wires, and officials refused to forward telegraph messages. In the initial chase after Villa, cavalry units were frequently out of touch with their headquarters, which is one reason why the pursuit was so disjointed. Only after diplomatic negotiations forced Pershing into a holding pattern did field wireless equipment begin to stitch the operation together but, by then, to no real purpose. (Courtesy Carter Rila Collection.)

Field artillery aerographers sent up 30-gram balloons filled with hydrogen or helium to track winds at different elevations up to 20,000 feet. By using the 8-power telescope at right, the soldiers could apply arithmetic formulas to wind patterns and adjust the direction and trajectory of artillery fire. (Courtesy Carter Rila Collection.)

New rolling kitchens, modeled after the German examples, could feed up to 150 men per unit. The soldiers griped, but their menus featured traditional American fare—scrambled eggs, bacon, roast beef and potatoes, hamburgers—supplemented by an occasional dish with a French-sounding name, which is not to say how this food tasted. (Courtesy Carter Rila Collection.)

Hiram Stevens Maxim invented the world's first automatic machine gun (as opposed to a mechanical machine gun such as the Gatling) in 1882. This 1904 Maxim mode, .30-06 caliber, was standard in the U.S. Army through World War I. U.S. soldiers nicknamed it the "Belgian Rattlesnake," and the Germans employed the identical gun. (Courtesy Andreas Brown Collection.)

When the mobilization occurred along the border, the army owned few medium field pieces, such as this 4.7-inch gun M1906. It was later slightly converted to allow it to utilize supplies of French 120-mm ammunition. The gun weighed 2,688 pounds on its steel-tired wheels and 8,068 pounds when braced in firing position. (Courtesy Andreas Brown Collection.)

OBSERVATION LADDER.

How did the army spot for its artillery? It ordered a soldier up an observation ladder. This practice worked fine in training exercises, but in combat . . . . (Courtesy John Hardman Collection.)

OBSERVATION LADDER IN USE.

Another artillery observer, this time "camou-
flaged" as a tree. (Courtesy John Hardman
Collection.)

Border ground conditions led the army to recognize the value of tractors with treads. From there, it was but a short step to armored cars with treads—or tanks. (Courtesy Carter Rila Collection.)

Here is how motor power came to replace horse power: a single, powerful tractor could pull a long line of wagons loaded with pontoons for bridge building. Formerly, each wagon had to be hauled by its own team of mules or horses.
(Courtesy Carter Rila Collection.)

Motorized military ambulances, employed for the first time in Mexico, received mixed efficiency reports. They may have carried wounded men back to Columbus faster than horse-drawn transport, but en route the jouncing caused by the deeply pitted and rutted roads often aggravated the injuries of the soldiers, and even cracked a few formerly sound ribs. Still, the truck ambulances, which carried eight seated patients, must have been better than the motorcycles, which carried two patients in stretchers at speeds of up to sixty miles an hour. (Courtesy El Paso Public Library.)

As skirmishes and accidents claimed more and more lives, the funeral cortège, accompanied by full military honors, became a regular sight on El Paso's thoroughfares. (Courtesy Carter Rila Collection.)

Anáres Garcia   Gen. Obregon   Gen. Bell

Neither Wilson nor Carranza said they wanted war, although a good many of their generals did. A tenuous peace was maintained through negotiations at which the U.S. sought guarantees for its interests in Mexico and the Mexicans meant to drive a hard bargain in exchange. Many of the negotiators had for years both formally and informally worked out border differences. The men had become good acquaintances, if not friends—for example these ranking military negotiators: Andrés García, a Constitutionalist; Alvaro Obregón, Carranza's top general, and Major General George Bell, El Paso District Military Commander. (Courtesy John Hardman Collection.)

The bombast of Theodore Roosevelt, aspiring to reelection to the presidency in 1916 on the Progressive ticket, further complicated Wilson's negotiations. In regard to a Mexican policy, Roosevelt admonished Wilson that "a weakling who fears to stand up manfully for the right may work as much mischief as any strong-armed wrong-doer." As for the Pershing expedition, he charged that Wilson had launched it "in the interest of one bandit chief whom at the moment he liked in order to harm one other bandit chief whom at the moment he disliked." (Courtesy Roger Bowman Collection.)

CARRANZA'S TROOPS.

Carranza's army was a patchquilt of ambitious generals and ranking officers in search of power and personal gain, along with troops of common Mexicans who had not much better to go home to. As victory in the civil war neared, more and more Mexicans joined the Constitutionalists in order to claim the fruits of the revolution. (Courtesy John Hardman Collection.)

No less opportunistic were Sonora's Yaqui Indians. They fought with a variety of powerbrokers, selling their services as fierce warriors and wily scouts. (Courtesy John Hardman Collection.)

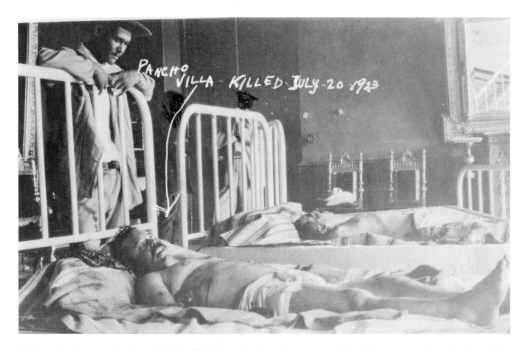

Villa, who in 1920 had traded his rifle for an hacienda, was murdered three years later in Parral in what was described as a local argument. The explanation has satisfied most historians, but conspiracy theorists still link the murder to high federal authorities, even the presidency. (Courtesy Andreas Brown Collection.)

• Notes •

Chapter One

1. Betty Lewis, *Monterey Bay Yesterday: A Nostalgic Era in Postcards* (Fresno, Calif.: Valley Publishers, 1977), p. vii; Sam Stark, "Keepsakes Series: Number One in a Series of Keepsakes," *West Coast Expositions and Galas* (The Book Club of California, 1970), p. 1.

2. Stark, "Keepsakes Series," p. 1.

3. Frank Staff, *The Picture Postcard and Its Origins* (New York: Frederick A. Praeger, 1966), p. 49. Measuring five and one-eighth by three inches, the cards were made of good, stiff paper with a one-cent stamp printed in the upper right-hand corner. The cream-colored postal had brown velvet printing in the upper left-hand corner: "United States Postal Card" and gave instructions, "Write the address only on this side—the message on the other." Three ruled lines provided for the address, with the top line preceded by the word "To." The back of the card, intended for communication, was completely plain. Absolutely no variation in size, shape, or color was permitted.

4. *Ibid.,* pp. 7, 86. The privately printed postcard in the United States actually antedates the government postal in either the America or Europe. What appears to have been the first one was copyrighted on December 17, 1861 by J. P. Charlton of Philadelphia and published by H. L. Lipman of the same city. The cards have blank message sides, and the backs have three lines for the address, a stamp box, and the words "Copy-right received 1861. Lipman's Postal Card-Patent applied for." Unfortunately, since existing postal regulations required that these cards be put into envelopes before being mailed, there was no real advantage to using them, and they never became popular. Thus, in a discussion of the evolution of the postcard, the Lipman card must be regarded as a dead end. See Dorothy B. Ryan, *Picture Postcards in the United States, 1893–1918* (1st ed., rev.; New York: Clarkson N. Potter, 1982), p. 1; Peter Collins, "War Nurtured Postcards: UPU Organizer Influenced Their Early Development," *Stamp Collector* (Nov. 11, 1985): 10.

5. Stark, "Keepsakes Series," p. 1.

6. Staff, *The Picture Postcard,* p. 7.

7. *Ibid.,* p. 61; Ryan, *Picture Postcards,* p. 2.

8. Ryan, *Picture Postcards,* pp. 2–3; Staff, *The Picture Postcard,* p. 61.

9. Ryan, *Picture Postcards,* p. 2; Staff, *The Picture Postcard,* p. 62.

10. Hal Morgan and Andreas Brown, *Prairie Fires and Paper Moons: The American Photographic Postcard: 1900–1920* (Boston: David R. Godine, 1981), p. 187; Staff, *The Picture Postcard,* p. 62.

11. *Information Please Almanac, Atlas and Yearbook: 1970* (New York: Dan Golenpaul Associates, 1969), p. 622; Morgan and Brown, *Prairie Fires,* p. xiii.

12. Morgan and Brown, *Prairie Fires,* p. xiii.

13. Ryan, *Picture Postcards,* pp. 15–16.

14. Philip L. Condax and Andrew H. Eskind, private interview held at International Museum of Photography at George Eastman House, Rochester, N.Y., June 7, 1985.

15. Beaumont Newhall, *The History of Photography from 1839 to the Present Day* (New York: The Museum of Modern Art, 1964), p. 88.

16. Condax and Eskind, private interview, June 7, 1985; Newhall, *The History of Photography,* p. 88; Morgan and Brown, *Prairie Fires,* p. xiii.

17. Morgan and Brown, *Prairie Fires,* p. xiv.

18. See *Ibid.*

19. Lewis, *Monterey Bay Yesterday,* p. vii; Stark, "Keepsake Series," p. 2; Morgan and Brown, *Prairie Fires,* p. 187.

20. These cards are today among the most sought after by collectors and are, therefore, among the most valuable. They also provide the best historical records available of the nation's town-planning and architectural past.

21. See Morgan and Brown, *Prairie Fires,* p. xiii–xiv.

22. Eastman Kodak Company, *Kodak Trade Circular* (May 1910): 7–8.

23. Ryan, *Picture Postcards,* p. 22.

24. *Ibid.,* pp. 16, 22–25.

25. Staff, *The Picture Postcard,* p. 49.

26. George Fitch, "Upon the Threatened Extinction of the Art of Letter Writing," *The American Magazine* (June 1910): 172–73.

27. Ryan, *Picture Postcards,* pp. 33, 61–68, 70, 87, 89, 91, 100–103, 105–11, 117–23, 127, 145, 151, 165–85, 207, 221; Staff, *The Picture Postcard,* pp. 67–80.

28. Ryan, *Picture Postcards,* pp. 27–32.

29. *Ibid.,* pp. 90, 115.

30. See *Moving Picture World* (June 20, 1914): 1638; *Moving Picture World,* (July 18, 1914): 387; Andreas Brown, private interview held at Gotham Book Mart, New York City, April 20, 1985; Stark, "Keepsake Series," p. 2.

31. Postcard in collection of D. J. Sobery, Seabrook, Tex.

32. Postcard in collection of John O. Hardman, Warren, Ohio.

33. Jim Dan Hill, *The Minute Man in Peace and War: A History of the National Guard* (Harrisburg, Pa.: The Stackpole Company, 1964), pp. 230–35; Leon C. Metz, *Fort Bliss: An Illustrated History* (El Paso, Tex.: Mangan Books, 1981), p. 71.

34. Roger Batchelder, *Watching and Waiting on the Border* (Boston: Houghton Mifflin Company, 1917), p. 95; Hill, *The Minute Man,* pp. 242, 248; Tracey Hammond Lewis, *Along the Rio Grand* (New York: Lewis Publishing Company, 1916), p. 18; Floyd P. Gibbons, *How the Laconia Sank: The Militia Mobilization on the Mexican Border* (Chicago: Daughaday and Company, 1917), pp. 45–56, 90.

35. Postcard in collection of John O. Hardman, Warren, Ohio.

36. *Ibid.*

37. Postcard in collection of El Paso Public Library, El Paso, Tex.

38. Postcard in collection of John O. Hardman, Warren, Ohio.

39. Postcard in Jodie P. Harris Postcard Collection, Archives of the Big Bend, Sul Ross State University, Alpine, Tex.

40. A leading private collector of "Mexican War Post Cards," John O. Hardman, has identified postcards in his collection made by one hundred different firms and individuals. John O. Hardman, private interview held in Warren, Ohio, Sept. 15, 1985.

41. Letter, Walter H. Horne to Mrs. Henry Horne and Edward Horne, El Paso, Tex., March 21, 1916, El Paso Public Library, W. H. Horne Letter File.

42. Letter, Walter H. Horne to Mrs. Henry Horne, El Paso, Tex., Aug. 4, 1916, El Paso Public Library, W. H. Horne Letter File.

43. Ryan, *Picture Postcards,* pp. 146, 327. See Ed Davis, "Collecting 'Old Auto' Postcards," *Postcard Collector* (March 1985): 50.

44. Metz, *Fort Bliss,* p. 74.

45. Hill, *The Minute Man,* p. 242.

Chapter Two

1. Certain details concerning the life of Walter H. Horne that are not directly relevant to his career as a postcard photographer have been omitted from this chapter but are discussed in an excellent article on Horne by Mary A. Sarber, "W. H. Horne and the Mexican War Photo Postcard Company," *Password* 31 (Spring 1986): 5–15.

2. Letter, Katherine H. Snell, Head Librarian, Hubbard Free Library, to Mary A. Sarber, Hallowell, Maine, Sept. 12, 1984, El Paso Public Library, W. H. Horne Letter File; Rose A. Gilpatrick, "Old Loudon Hill," in *Historic Hallowell,* ed. by Katherine H. Snell and Vincent P. Ledew (Hallowell, Maine: Hallowell Bicentennial Committee, 1962), pp. 72–73; *El Paso Morning Times,* Oct. 15, 1921; *Kennebec Journal,* Oct. 18, 1921.

3. Letter, Walter H. Horne to Edward Horne, New York, N.Y., Feb. 4, 1905, El Paso Public Library, W. H. Horne Letter File.

4. Jeffery R. M. Kunz, ed., *The American Medical Association Family Medical Guide* (New York: Random House, 1982), pp. 563–64; Joseph J. Previte, *Human Physiology* (New York: McGraw-Hill Book Company, 1983), p. 484.

5. Letter, Walter H. Horne to Edward Horne, Los Angeles, Calif., Oct. 13, 1909, El Paso Public Library, W. H. Horne Letter File.

6. Letter, Walter H. Horne to Edward Horne, El Paso, Tex., Feb. 26, 1910, El Paso Public Library, W. H. Horne Letter File.

7. *Ibid.*

8. Metz, *Fort Bliss: An Illustrated History,* p. 59; Tracey Hammond Lewis, *Along the Rio Grand* (New York: Lewis Publishing Company, 1916), pp. 6, 17.

9. Letter, Walter H. Horne to Edward Horne, El Paso, Tex., Feb. 26, 1910, El Paso Public Library, W. H. Horne Letter File; Letter, Walter H. Horne to Mr. and Mrs. Henry Horne, El Paso, Tex., Feb. 5, 1911, El Paso Public Library, W. H. Horne Letter File; Letter, Walter H. Horne to Gertrude Horne, El Paso, Tex., Feb. 11, 1911, El Paso Public Library, W. H. Horne Letter File.

10. Letter, Walter H. Horne to Gertrude Horne, El Paso, Tex., Feb. 11, 1911, El Paso Public Library, W. H. Horne Letter File. See Shawn Lay, *War, Revolution, and the Ku Klux Klan* (El Paso, Tex.: Texas Western Press, 1985), pp. 18–19.

11. See Postcard, Walter H. Horne to Mrs. Henry Horne, El Paso, Tex., May 8, 1911, El Paso Public Library, W. H. Horne Postcard Collection; Postcard, Walter H. Horne to Gertrude Horne, El Paso, Tex., May 20, 1911, Collection of John O. Hardman, Warren, Ohio.

12. Postcard, Walter H. Horne to Mrs. Henry Horne, El Paso, Tex., May 8, 1911, El Paso Public Library, W. H. Horne Postcard Collection.

13. Postcard, Walter H. Horne to Gertrude Horne, El Paso, Tex., May 20, 1911, Collection of John O. Hardman, Warren, Ohio.

14. See Metz, *Fort Bliss,* p. 60; Letter, Walter H. Horne to Gertrude Horne, El Paso, Tex., Sept. 24, 1911, El Paso Public Library, W. H. Horne Letter File.

15. Postcard, Walter H. Horne to Mrs. Henry Horne, Trinidad, Colo., July 7, 1911, El Paso Public Library, W. H. Horne Postcard Collection; Letter, Walter H. Horne to Mr. and Mrs. Henry Horne, Trinidad, Colo., July 26, 1911, El Paso Public Library, W. H. Horne Letter File; Letter, Walter H. Horne to Mrs. Henry Horne, Los Cerrillos, N. Mex., Aug. 11, 1911, El Paso Public Library, W. H. Horne Letter File.

16. Letter, Walter H. Horne to Mr. and Mrs. Henry Horne, El Paso, Tex., Sept. 9, 1911, El Paso Public Library, W. H. Horne Letter File.

17. Letter, Walter H. Horne to Gertrude Horne, El Paso, Tex., Sept. 24, 1911, El Paso Public Library, W. H. Horne Letter File.

18. Letter, Walter H. Horne to Mr. and Mrs. Henry Horne, El Paso, Tex., Oct. 9, 1911, El Paso Public Library, W. H. Horne Letter File.

19. *Ibid.*

20. Letter, Walter H. Horne to Mr. and Mrs. Henry Horne, El Paso, Tex., Dec. 20, 1911, El Paso Public Library, W. H. Horne Letter File.

21. Letter, Walter H. Horne to Mr. and Mrs. Henry Horne, El Paso, Tex., Apr. 14, 1912, El Paso Public Library, W. H. Horne Letter File.

22. Metz, *Fort Bliss,* pp. 59, 60; Letter, Walter H. Horne to Mr. and Mrs. Henry Horne, El Paso, Tex., Sept. 30, 1912, El Paso Public Library, W. H. Horne Letter File.

23. Letter, Walter H. Horne to Mr. and Mrs. Henry Horne, El Paso, Tex., Sept. 30, 1912, El Paso Public Library, W. H. Horne Letter File.

24. Postcard, Walter H. Horne to Gertrude Horne, El Paso, Tex., Oct. 25, 1912, El Paso Public Library, W. H. Horne Postcard Collection; Postcard, Walter H. Horne to Mrs. Henry Horne, El Paso, Tex., Oct. 26, 1912, El Paso Public Library, W. H. Horne Postcard Collection; Postcard, Walter H. Horne to Mrs. Henry Horne, El Paso, Tex., May 13, 1913, El Paso Public Library, W. H. Horne Postcard Collection; Postcard, Walter H. Horne to Mrs. Henry Horne, El Paso, Tex., Nov. 11, 1913, El Paso Public Library, W. H. Horne Postcard Collection.

25. Postcard, Walter H. Horne to Gertrude Horne, El Paso, Tex., Nov. 24, 1913, Collection of Carter Rila, Gaithersburg, Md.

26. Postcard, Walter H. Horne to Gertrude Horne, El Paso, Tex., Dec. 25, 1913, El Paso Public Library, W. H. Horne Postcard Collection.

27. Letter, Walter H. Horne to Gertrude Horne, El Paso, Tex., Jan. 18, 1914, El Paso Public Library, W. H. Horne Letter File.

28. Postcard, Walter H. Horne to Gertrude Horne, El Paso, Tex., Apr. 2, 1914, Collection of Carter Rila, Gaithersburg, Md.; Postcard, Walter H. Horne to Mr. and Mrs. Henry Horne, El Paso, Tex., Apr. 6, 1914, Collection of Carter Rila, Gaithersburg, Md.

29. Philip C. Geraci, *Photojournalism: Making Pictures for Publication* (2nd ed.; Dubuque, Iowa: Kendall-Hart Publishing Company, 1980), p. 56; Philip L. Condax and Andrew H. Eskind, private interview held at International Museum of Photography at George Eastman House, Rochester, N.Y., June 7, 1985.

30. Letter, Walter H. Horne to Mr. and Mrs. Henry Horne, El Paso, Tex., May 12, 1914, El Paso Public Library, W. H. Horne Letter File.

31. See Postcard, Walter H. Horne to Gertrude Horne, El Paso, Tex., Oct. 15, 1914, Collection of Carter Rila, Gaithersburg, Md.; Walter H. Horne to Gertrude Horne, El Paso, Tex., Oct. 27, 1914, El Paso Public Library, W. H. Horne Postcard Collection; Letter, Walter H. Horne to Mr. and Mrs. Henry Horne, El Paso, Tex., Feb. 19, 1915, El Paso Public Library, W. H. Horne Letter File; Postcard, Walter H. Horne to Gertrude Horne, El Paso, Tex., Nov. 18, 1915, El Paso Public Library, W. H. Horne Postcard Collection.

32. Letter, Walter H. Horne to Mr. and Mrs. Henry Horne, El Paso, Tex., July 17, 1914, El Paso Public Library, W. H. Horne Letter File; Letter, Walter H. Horne to Mr. and Mrs. Henry Horne, El Paso, Tex., Aug. 18, 1915, El Paso Public Library, W. H. Horne Letter File.

33. Postcard, Walter H. Horne to Gertrude Horne, El Paso, Tex., Dec. 3, 1915, El Paso Public Library, W. H. Horne Postcard Collection.

34. See Letter, Walter H. Horne to Mr. and Mrs. Henry Horne, El Paso, Tex., Dec. 17, 1914, El Paso Public Library, W. H. Horne Letter File.

35. *El Paso Morning Times, Edición en Español,* Jan. 16, 1916. Also see Brown Meggs, *The War Train: A Novel of 1916* (New York: Atheneum, 1981), pp. 318–22; Postcard, Walter H. Horne to Edward Horne, El Paso, Tex., Jan. 16, 1916, El Paso Public Library, W. H. Horne Postcard Collection; Postcard, Walter H. Horne to Gertrude Horne, El Paso, Tex., Jan. 16, 1916, Collection of Carter Rila, Gaithersburg, Md.; Lewis, *Along the Rio Grand,* p. 18.

36. Postcard, Walter H. Horne to Gertrude Horne, El Paso, Tex., Mar. 15, 1916, El Paso Public Library, W. H. Horne Postcard Collection.

37. Letter, Walter H. Horne to Mrs. Henry Horne and Edward Horne, El Paso, Tex., Mar. 21, 1916, El Paso Public Library, W. H. Horne Letter File; C. Tucker Beckett, "Albums: C. Tucker Beckett's Photographs of the Mexican Expedition, U.S. Army 1916," unnumbered preface, in Record Group 165-CB, Still Pictures Branch, National Archives of the United States, Washington, D.C. While Horne may have traveled by automobile to Columbus with other El Paso photographers, it is clear that by "we" in his letter of March 21, 1916, he refers to himself and an employee and not to himself and other photographers, who, after all, were his competitors.

38. *New York Times,* Mar. 15, 1916; Mar. 16, 1916; Mar. 23, 1916. See Record Group 165-MP, Still Pictures Branch, National Archives of the United States, Washington, D.C.

39. C. Tucker Beckett, "Albums: C. Tucker Beckett's Photographs of the Mexican Expedition, U.S. Army, 1916," unnumbered preface, in Record Group 165-CB, Still Pictures Branch, National Archives of the United States, Washington, D.C.; C. Tucker Beckett, "Military Photography in Mexico," *The Camera* (Nov. 1916): 599–608; *El Paso Herald,* May 1, 1916.

40. Lewis, *Along the Rio Grand,* p. 18.

41. Postcard, Walter H. Horne to R. J. Deming, El Paso, Tex., May 6, 1916, Collection of John O. Hardman, Warren, Ohio.

42. Postcard, Walter Horne to Mrs. Henry

Horne, El Paso, Tex., July 19, 1916, El Paso Public Library, W. H. Horne Postcard Collection.

43. Letter, Walter H. Horne to Mrs. Henry Horne, El Paso, Tex., Aug. 4, 1916, El Paso Public Library, W. H. Horne Letter File.

44. Letter, Walter H. Horne to Mrs. Henry Horne, El Paso, Tex., June 26, 1916, El Paso Public Library, W. H. Horne Letter File.

45. See Postcard, Walter Horne to Edward Horne, El Paso, Tex., n.d., El Paso Public Library, W. H. Horne Postcard Collection.

46. See *El Paso Morning Times,* Apr. 4, 1916; Apr. 6, 1916; Apr. 8, 1916.

47. See *Moving Picture World,* June 10, 1911, p. 1304; Kevin Brownlow, *The War, the West and the Wilderness* (New York: Alfred A. Knopf, 1979), p. 90.

48. Brownlow, *The War, the West and the Wilderness,* pp. 91, 96, 101–2.

49. See *Moving Picture World,* June 20, 1914, p. 1639; June 27, 1914, p. 1863; July 18, 1914, p. 396.

50. *Ibid.,* June 20, 1914, p. 1639.

51. See, for example, *ibid.,* Aug. 15, 1914, pp. 916, 1012, 1016; Jan. 1, 1916, pp. 20, 35; Jan. 8, 1916, pp. 182, 198; Jan. 15, 1916, p. 481; Feb. 5, 1916, p. 859; Feb. 19, 1916, pp. 1073, 1090; Mar. 4, 1916, p. 1564; Mar. 11, 1916, p. 1706.

52. *Ibid.,* Apr. 1, 1916, p. 149.

53. *Ibid.,* Apr. 15, 1916, p. 506.

54. *Ibid.,* Apr. 1, 1916, p. 149; *El Paso Morning Times,* Apr. 4, 1916.

55. Richard Polese, ed., "Assignment: Villa Raid, Excerpts from the Journal of Harold Palmer Brown," *El Palacio: Magazine of the Museum of New Mexico* 86 (Fall 1980): 14; Philip L. Condax and Andrew H. Eskind, private interview held at International Museum of Photography at George Eastman House, Rochester, N.Y., June 7, 1985.

56. See Postcard, Walter H. Horne to Gertrude Horne, El Paso, Tex., Apr. 11, 1918, El Paso Public Library, W. H. Horne Postcard Collection; Postcard, Walter H. Horne to Gertrude Horne, El Paso, Tex., Jan. 16, 1919, El Paso Public Library, W. H. Horne Postcard Collection; Walter H. Horne to Gertrude Horne, El Paso, Tex., June 24, 1919, El Paso Public Library, W. H. Horne Postcard Collection; Postcard, Walter H. Horne to Gertrude Horne, El Paso, Tex., July 28, 1919, El Paso Public Library, W. H. Horne Postcard Collection.

57. Letter, Walter H. Horne to Mrs. Henry Horne, El Paso, Tex., Aug. 19, 1917, El Paso Public Library, W. H. Horne Letter File.

58. Letter, Edward Horne to Ethel Marston, El Paso, Tex., Oct. 9, 1921, El Paso Public Library, W. H. Horne Letter File.

59. *El Paso Morning Times,* Oct. 15, 1921; *Kennebec Journal,* Oct. 18, 1921.

60. Last Will and Testament of Walter H. Horne, El Paso, Tex., Oct. 10, 1921, El Paso Public Library, W. H. Horne Letter File; Marriage Certificate of Walter H. Horne and Adelina Zuvia, El Paso, Tex., July 21, 1921, El Paso Public Library, W. H. Horne Letter File.

Chapter Three

1. Professor Vanderwood is working on a book about the people of Papigochic. His conclusions are based on his research in the local archives of the region. See also: Michael C. Meyer, *Mexican Rebel: Pascual Orozco and the Mexican Revolution* (Lincoln: University of Nebraska Press, 1967), pp. 14–15.

2. For a brief overview on Díaz dictatorship see: Paul J. Vanderwood, *Disorder and Progress: Bandits, Police and Mexican Development* (Lincoln: University of Nebraska Press, 1981), especially Parts 2–4. For special topics, consult the bibliography.

3. Don M. Coerver and Linda B. Hall, *Texas and the Mexican Revolution: A Study in State and National Border Policy, 1910–1920* (San Antonio: Trinity University Press, 1984), pp. 7–16; Rodolfo Rocha, "The Influence of the Mexican Revolution on the Mexico-Texas Border, 1910–1916" (Ph.D. dissertation, Texas Tech University, 1981), and James A. Sandos, "The Mexican Revolution and the United States, 1915–1917: The Impact of Conflict on the Tamaulipas-Texas Frontier upon the Emergence of Revolutionary Government in Mexico (Ph.D. dissertation, University of California, Berkeley, 1978).

4. Vanderwood, *Disorder and Progress,* Chap. 13; Thomas H. Russell, *Mexico in Peace and War: A Narrative of Mexican History and Conditions from the Earliest Times to the Present Hour, Including an Account of the Military Operations by the United States at Vera Cruz in 1914 and the Causes that Led Thereto* (Chicago: Reilly & Britton, 1914), pp. 306–7.

5. P. Edward Haley, *Revolution and Intervention: The Diplomacy of Taft and Wilson with Mexico, 1910–1917* (Cambridge, Mass.: Massachusetts Institute of Technology Press, 1970), p. 14.

6. Customs issues are discussed in Michael D. Carman, *United States Customs and the Madero Revolution* (El Paso: Texas Western Press, 1976). See also: Haley, *Revolution and Intervention,* pp. 21–33. For U.S. attitudes toward radical Mexican dissidents along the border, see William D. Raat, *Revoltosos: Mexico's Rebels in the United States, 1903–1923* (College Station: Texas A & M Press, 1981).

7. John Patrick Finnegan, *Against the Specter of a Dragon: The Campaign for American Military Preparedness, 1914–1917* (Westport, Conn.: Greenwood Press, 1974), p. 6; William M. Pratt, "On the Border with Our Army," *New England Magazine* (July–August 1911): 596; Kitty Barry, "Pitching Camp for Twenty-Thousand: An Observer's Impression of the Arrival of our Troops in Texas," *Harper's Weekly* (April 1, 1911): 9; Jack C. Lane, *Armed Progressive: General Leonard Wood* (San Rafael, Calif.: Presidio Press, 1978), pp. 169–71.

8. Barry, "Pitching Camp," p. 9.

9. Rocha, "Mexico-Texas Border," pp. 81–82; Pratt, "Border with Our Army," pp. 30–36; George B. Rodney, *As a Cavalryman Remembers* (Caldwell, Idaho: Caxton Printers, 1944), pp. 236–41.

10. Oscar J. Martínez, *Fragments of the Mexican Revolution: Personal Accounts from the Border* (Albuquerque: University of New Mexico Press, 1983), p. 130; Dale F. Beecher, "Incentive to Violence: Political Exploitations of Lawlessness on the United States–Mexico Border, 1866–1886" (Ph.D. dissertation, University of Utah, 1982), pp. iv–v; Charles Harris and Louis R. Sadler, "The Underside of the Mexican Revolution: El Paso, 1912," *The Americas* 39 (July 1982): 69–82; Rocha, "Mexico-Texas Border," pp. 103–4, 116–17; Major Edward S. O'Reilly, *Roving and Fighting: Adventures under Four Flags* (London: T. Werner Laurie, Ltd., 1918), p. 269.

11. Martínez, *Fragments,* pp. 83–84; Don M. Coerver and Linda B. Hall, "The Arizona-Sonora Border and the Mexican Revolution, 1910–1920," *Journal of the West* 24 (April 1985): 77–78; Rocha, "Mexico-Texas Border," pp. 122–23.

12. All comments on photo postcards, including their messages quoted below, refer to the collection of postcards assembled for this book. The source of each card published in this volume is noted beneath the respective card in the photo sections.

13. Coerver and Hall, *Texas and the Mexican Revolution,* pp. 24–27.

14. Martínez, *Fragments,* identification of photo between pp. 97–98.

15. Martínez, *Fragments,* pp. 132–33.

16. Sandos, "Impact of Conflict," p. 245.

17. Vanderwood, *Disorder and Progress,* Chap. 14.

18. For Madero, see Stanley R. Ross, *Francisco I. Madero: Apostle of Mexican Democracy* (New York: Columbia University Press, 1955) and David G. LaFrance, "A People Betrayed: Francisco I. Madero and the Mexican Revolution in Puebla (Ph.D. dissertation, Indiana University, 1984); for Orozco: Meyer, *Pascual Orozco* (Lincoln: University of Nebraska Press, 1967); for Zapata: John Womack, *Zapata and the Mexican Revolution* (New York: Knopf, 1969); for the radical liberals: Lowell L. Blaisdell, *The Desert Revolution: Baja California, 1911* (Madison: University of Wisconsin Press, 1962); for Huerta: Michael C. Meyer, *Huerta: A Political Portrait* (Lincoln: University of Nebraska Press, 1972); for revolutionary activity in Chihuahua: Francisco R. Almada, *La Revolución en el estado de Chihuahua,* 2 vols. (México: Biblioteca del Instituto Nacional de Estúdios Históricos de la Revolución Mexicana, 1964); for the same in Sonora: Hector Aguilar Camín, *La Frontera nomada: Sonora y la Revolución Mexicana* (México: El Siglo Veintiuno, 1977).

19. Sandos, "Impact of Conflict," pp. 232–35; Haley, *Revolution and Intervention,* Chaps. 5–6; Mark T. Gilderhus, *Diplomacy and Revolution: U.S.-Mexican Relations under Wilson and Carranza* (Tucson: University of Arizona Press, 1977), pp. ix–xii.

20. Charles C. Cumberland, *Mexican Revolution: The Constitutionalist Years* (Austin: University of Texas Press, 1972); Kenneth J. Grieb, *The United States and Huerta* (Lincoln: University of Nebraska Press, 1969).

21. Friedrich Katz, *The Secret War in Mexico: Europe, the United States and the Mexican Revolution* (Chicago: University of Chicago Press, 1981); Meyer *Huerta,* pp. 88, 98–99.

22. Rocha, "Mexico-Texas Border," p. 145–49.

23. Joseph R. Monticone, "Revolutionary Mexico and the U.S. Southwest: The Columbus Raid" (M.A.

thesis, California State University, Fullerton, 1981), p. 34; Rocha, "Mexico-Texas Border," p. 161; O'Reilly, *Roving and Fighting,* pp. 297–98.

24. Kevin Brownlow, *The War, the West, and the Wilderness* (New York: Knopf, 1974), pp. 84–105.

25. Sandos, "Impact of Conflict," p. 234.

26. Haley, *Revolution and Intervention,* pp. 162–63; Sandos, "Impact of Conflict," p. 235.

27. John Hart, "American Landholding and the Crisis of the Porfirian Political Economy," paper delivered at the VII Reunión de Historiadores Mexicanos y Norteamericanos, 22–26 Octubre 1985, Oaxaca, México.

28. Larry D. Hill, *Emissaries to a Revolution: Woodrow Wilson's Executive Agents in Mexico* (Baton Rouge: Louisiana State University Press, 1974); Haley, *Revolution and Intervention,* Chaps. 5–6; and John M. Hart, *Revolutionary Mexico: The Coming and Process of the Mexican Revolution* (Berkeley: University of California Press, 1987). Our gratitude is extended to Professor Hart for allowing us to read his fine book in manuscript form.

29. Robert E. Quirk, *An Affair of Honor: Woodrow Wilson and the Occupation of Veracruz* (New York: W. W. Norton, 1962); Haley, *Revolution and Intervention,* Chap. 7. For a succinct treatment of the Veracruz affair from the Mexican point of view see: Andrea Martínez, *La Intervención norteamericana: Veracruz, 1914* (México: Secretaría de Educación Pública, 1982).

30. See note 12.

31. Photo postcards in the collection of John Hardman, Warren, Ohio.

32. Photo postcards in the collection of Andreas Brown, New York, N.Y.

33. Photo postcards in the collection of Andreas Brown, New York, N.Y.

34. Photo postcards in the collection of John Hardman, Warren, Ohio.

35. Katz, *Secret War,* Chap. 9.

36. Coerver and Hall, *Texas and the Mexican Revolution,* pp. 112–16; Haley, *Revolution and Intervention,* Chap. 8.

37. Charles Harris and Louis R. Sadler, "The Plan of San Diego and the Mexican–United States War Crisis of 1916: A Reexamination," *Hispanic American Historical Review* 58 (August 1978): 381–408; Rocha, "Mexico-Texas Border," pp. 262–318; Martínez, *Fragments,* pp. 137–70.

38. Quoted in Coerver and Hall, *Texas and the Mexican Revolution,* p. 106; Martínez, *Fragments,* pp. 171–72.

39. Quoted in Coerver and Hall, *Texas and the Mexican Revolution,* p. 106.

40. Quoted in Coerver and Hall, *Texas and the Mexican Revolution,* p. 107–8; Martínez, *Fragments,* pp. 173–76.

41. Rocha, "Mexico-Texas Border," pp. 332–33; Frank Cushman Pierce, *A Brief History of the Rio Grande* (Menash, Wis.: George Banta Publishing Company, 1917), pp. 103, 114.

42. Sandos, "Impact of Conflict," p. 164.

43. Coerver and Hall, *Texas and the Mexican Revolution,* p. 107.

44. Sandos, "Impact of Conflict," pp. 5 and 145; Pierce, *Lower Rio Grande,* pp. 112, 115, 128.

45. Harris and Sadler, "Plan of San Diego," pp. 387–406.

46. Frederich Katz, "Pancho Villa and the Attack on Columbus, New Mexico," *American Historical Review* 83 (February 1978): 101–30; Hugh L. Scott, *Some Memories of a Soldier* (New York: Century Co., 1928), p. 517; O'Reilly, *Roving and Fighting,* p. 318.

47. Clarence C. Clendenen, *Blood on the Border: The United States Army and the Mexican Irregulars* (New York: Macmillan, 1969), pp. 186–89; Martínez, *Fragments,* pp. 70–74; Coerver and Hall, "The Arizona-Sonora Border and the Mexican Revolution, 1910–1920," *Journal of the West* 24 (April 1985): 80–81.

Chapter Four

The Columbus raid has been well studied by both professional and popular historians, which does not mean that there is consensus about the event, especially its causes. For examples see: Charles Harris and Louis R. Sadler, "Pancho Villa and the Columbus Raid: The Missing Documents," *New Mexico Historical Review* 50 (October 1975): 335–46; Frederich Katz, "Pancho Villa," pp. 101–30; James A. Sandos, "German Involvement in Northern Mexico, 1915–1916: A New Look at the Columbus Raid," *Hispanic American Historical Review* 50 (February 1970): 70–89; E. Bruce White, "The Muddied Waters of Columbus, New Mexico," *The Americas* 32 (July 1975): 72–92; Francis J. Munch, "Villa's Columbus Raid: Practical Politics or German Design?," *New Mexico Historical Review* 44 (July 1969): 189–214; Herbert Molloy Mason, Jr., *The Great Pursuit* (New York: Random House, 1970), Chap. 1; Clarence Clendenen, *Blood on the Border,* Chap. 10; Joseph R. Monticone, "Revolutionary Mexico."

2. "Our Unpreparedness Revealed by Villa," *The Literary Digest* (1 April 1916): 883.

3. Frank Tompkins, *Chasing Villa: The Story Behind the Story of Chasing Villa into Mexico* (Harrisburg, Pa.: Military Service Publishing Company, 1939), pp. 47, 53, 56–57; Mason, *Great Pursuit,* p. 20; Monticone, "Revolutionary Mexico," p. 77.

4. See note 12, preceding section.

5. Monticone, "Revolutionary Mexico," discusses the various themes surrounding the causes of Villa's assault on Columbus. For more detailed information see note 1, above.

6. J. Ralph Randolph, "Border Reaction to the

Villa Raids," *West Texas Historical Association Year Book* 49 (1973): 12–13; Metz, *Fort Bliss: An Illustrated History,*)p. 68; Shawn Lay, *War, Revolution and the Ku Klux Klan* (El Paso: Texas Western Press, 1985), pp. 16, 25–26.

7. Monticone, "Revolutionary Mexico," pp. 69–72.

8. S. D. Lovell, *The Presidential Election of 1916* (Carbondale: Southern Illinois University Press, 1980), pp. 6–8; Monticone, "Revolutionary Mexico," pp. 84–85; Richard Goldhurst, *Pipeclay and Drill: John J. Pershing, the Classic American Soldier* (New York: Reader's Digest Press, 1977), p. 195.

9. Gilderhus, *Diplomacy and Revolution*, pp. 36–39; Haley, *Revolution and Intervention*, Chap. 9; Clendenen, *Blood on the Border*, pp. 223–24; Mason, *Great Pursuit*, p. 188.

10. Quoted in *Current Opinion* (May 8, 1916): p. 306.

11. The literature on the Pershing expedition is vast, a good deal provided by the participants themselves, such as Tomkins, *Chasing Villa*, and Col. Harry A. Toulmin, *With Pershing in Mexico* (Harrisburg, Pa.: Military Service Publishing Company, 1935). Pershing's few comments are in his autobiography, John J. Pershing, *My Experiences in the World War*, 2 vols. (New York: Frederick A. Stokes, 1931), pp. 9–12. For secondary accounts see: Clarence C. Clendenen, *The United States and Pancho Villa: A Study in Unconventional Diplomacy* (Ithaca, N.Y.: Cornell University Press, 1961); Haldeen Braddy, *Pershing's Expedition in Mexico* (El Paso: Texas Western College Press, 1966); Mason, *Great Pursuit;* Donald Smythe, *Guerrilla Warrior: The Early Life of John J. Pershing* (New York: Scribner, 1973); Michael L. Tate, "Pershing's Punitive Expedition: Pursuer of Bandits or Presidential Panacea?," *The Americas* 32 (July 1975): 46–72; and Vernon L. Williams, *Lieutenant Patton and the Ameri-*

can Army in the Mexican Punitive Expedition, 1915–1916 (Austin: Presidial Press, 1983).

12. Smythe, *Guerrilla Warrior*, p. 269; Gregory Mason, "Our Army of Education in Mexico," *Outlook* (April 26, 1916): 951.

13. Tompkins, *Chasing Villa*, pp. 138–44.

14. Katz, *Secret War*, p. 302; Lovell, *Presidential Election*, p. 8; Richard Goldhurst, *Pipeclay and Drill*, p. 195; Smythe, *Guerrilla Warrior*, p. 266.

15. *Current Opinion* (May 8, 1916): 304–5.

16. Gilderhus, *Diplomacy and Revolution*, pp. 39, 47.

17. Finnegan, *Specter of a Dragon*, pp. 142, 155; Allan R. Millett and Peter Maslowski, *For the Common Defense: A Military History of the U.S.A.* (New York: Free Press, 1984).

18. *Current Opinion* (May 8, 1916): 306.

19. Mason, *Great Pursuit*, p. 143; Clendenen, *Blood on the Border*, p. 224; Rollin W. Hutchinson, Jr., "The Motor Versus the Mule in Uncle Sam's War Department," *The American Review of Reviews* (July 1913): 59–64.

20. Clendenen, *Blood on the Border*, pp. 224–25; "The Motor Truck in Mexico," *Literary Digest* (May 27, 1916): 1599.

21. Clendenen, *Blood on the Border*, p. 225; Norman M. Cary, "The Use of the Motor Vehicle in the United States Army, 1899–1939" (Ph.D. dissertation, University of Georgia, 1980), pp. 97–104; "Our Motor Truck Railway," *Literary Digest* (May 20, 1916): 1488.

22. Tompkins, *Chasing Villa*, Appendix C, pp. 246, 251; B. G. Chynoweth, "Personal recollections," dated October 24, 1967, History Research Collection, U.S. Army War College; Clendenen, *Blood on the Border*, pp. 323–25.

23. Clendenen, *Blood on the Border*, p. 326; Carey, "Use of the Motor Vehicle," pp. 66–67; Roger Batch-

elder, *Watching and Waiting on the Border* (Boston: Houghton Mifflin, 1917), p. 106.

24. Mason, *Great Pursuit,* p. 187; Clendenen, *Blood on the Border,* p. 226; Williams, *Patton,* p. 71.

25. Ronnie C. Tyler, "The Little Punitive Expedition in the Big Bend," *Southwestern Historical Quarterly* 78 (January 1975): 263–84; Clendenen, *Blood on the Border,* pp. 297–381.

26. Carey, "Use of the Motor Vehicle," pp. 69, 112–13; Clendenen, *Blood on the Border,* pp. 297, 333–34; Smythe, *Guerrilla Warrior,* p. 274.

27. Mason, *Great Pursuit,* p. 103.

28. Tompkins, *Chasing Villa,* Appendix B, p. 236; Clendenen, *Blood on the Border,* pp. 316–18.

29. Mason, *Great Pursuit,* p. 103; Tompkins, *Chasing Villa,* Appendix B, p. 237; Clendenen, *Blood on the Border,* pp. 226, 321.

30. Mason, *Great Pursuit,* pp. 117–18; Tompkins, *Chasing Villa,* Appendix B, pp. 240–43.

31. Tompkins, *Chasing Villa,* Appendix B, pp. 242–43.

32. Tompkins, *Chasing Villa,* Appendix A, pp. 231–35.

33. Charles H. Harris and Louis R. Sadler, "United States Government Archives and the Mexican Revolution: Some New Approaches," paper presented at the meeting of the Mexicanist Session, Conference on Latin American History, American Historical Association, Washington, D.C., 1982, pp. 8–9. These authors are now writing a book about U.S. intelligence activities along the border during the Mexican Revolution.

34. Tyler, "Little Punitive Expedition," pp. 271–91; Mason, *Great Pursuit,* pp. 169, 174; Rocha, "Mexico-Texas Border," pp. 326–28; Clendenen, *Blood on the Border,* pp. 279–81; Carlysle G. Raht, *The Romance of Davis Mountains and Big Bend Country* (Odessa, Tex.: Rahtbooks Company, 1919), pp. 350–57.

35. See note 34.

36. Mason, *Great Pursuit,* p. 206.

37. Coerver and Hall, *Texas and the Mexican Revolution,* p. 109.

38. Mason, *Great Pursuit,* pp. 208–11; Harris and Sadler, "Plan of San Diego," p. 401; Coerver and Hall, *Texas and the Mexican Revolution,* p. 105; Rodney, *Cavalryman,* pp. 276–78.

39. Coerver and Hall, *Texas and the Mexican Revolution,* p. 104; Mason, *Great Pursuit,* p. 202; Smythe, *Guerrilla Warrior,* p. 251.

40. "The Collapse of Our Militia," *Forum* (September 1916): 296; John A. Cuthins, *A Famous Command: The Richmond Light Infantry Blues* (Richmond: Garrett and Massie, 1934).

41. John Dos Passos, *Mr. Wilson's War* (New York: Doubleday, 1962), p. 186.

42. Frederick Reid, "Mobilizing the Flintlock Army,—An Object Lesson," *Sunset* (May 1916): Dos Passos, *Wilson's War,* p. 185–86.

43. Dos Passos, *Wilson's War,* p. 188; "Collapse of our Militia," p. 296.

44. Metz, *Fort Bliss,* p. 71; Daniel B. Strickler, *The Memoirs of Lieutenant Governor, Lieutenant General Daniel Bursk Stickler* (Lancaster, Pa.: [n.d.], 1972), p. 15.

45. Mason, *Great Pursuit,* pp. 221–22; Batchelder, *Watching and Waiting,* pp. 63, 77, 93, 95, 159–60; Metz, *Fort Bliss,* p. 63.

46. "What Our Men Eat in Mexico," *Literary Digest* (November 11, 1916): 1246.

47. Dos Passos, *Wilson's War,* p. 187.

48. Edley Craighill, *The Musketeers* (Lynchburg, Va.: J. P. Bell Co., 1931), pp. 176, 181.

49. Postcards in the collection of John Hardman, Warren, Ohio.

50. All comments on photo postcards, including their messages quoted below, refer to the collection of

postcards assembled for this book. The source of each card published in this volume is noted beneath the respective card in the photo sections.

51. Batchelder, *Watching and Waiting,* p. 201; Lt. Kenneth Gow, *Letters of a Soldier* (New York: Herbert B. Covert, 1920), p. 1251.

52. A group of these cartoon-style cards is published in Jodie P. Harris, "Protecting the Big Bend—A Guardsman's View," *Southwestern Historical Quarterly* 78 (January 1975): 292–302.

53. Batchelder, *Watching and Waiting,* p. 208.

54. Postcard in the collection of John Hardman, Warren, Ohio.; Batchelder, *Watching and Waiting,* pp. 95–96; George Brooke, III, *With the First City Troop on the Mexican Border* (Philadelphia: John C. Winston Company, 1917), *passim.*

55. Batchelder, *Watching and Waiting,* pp. 95–96.

56. Harris and Sadler, "Plan of San Diego," pp. 392–93; Tompkins, *Chasing Villa,* summed up the sentiments of the military, p. 184; Smythe, *Guerrilla Warrior,* pp. 245–46.

57. Mason, *Great Pursuit,* pp. 223–28; Katz, *Secret War,* pp. 308–9; Clendenen, *Blood on the Border,* pp. 337–38.

58. Gilderhus, *Diplomacy and Revolution,* pp. 53–58; Mason, *Great Pursuit,* pp. 223–38; Katz, *Secret War,* pp. 308–9; Clendenen, *Blood on the Border,* pp. 337–38; Tompkins, *Chasing Villa,* pp. 215–16.

59. Gilderhus, *Diplomacy and Revolution,* p. 51.

Selected Bibliography

I. Books

Aguilar Camín, Hector. *La Frontera nomada: Sonora y la revolución mexicana*. México: El Siglo Veintiuno, 1977.

Almada, Francisco R. *La Revolución en el estado de Chihuahua*. 2 vols. México: Biblioteca del Instituto Nacional de Estudios Históricos de la Revolución Mexicana, 1964.

Batchelder, Roger. *Watching and Waiting on the Border*. Boston: Houghton, Mifflin, 1917.

Blaisdell, Lowell L. *The Desert Revolution: Baja California, 1911*. Madison: University of Wisconsin Press, 1962.

Braddy, Haldeen. *Pershing's Expedition in Mexico*. El Paso: Texas Western College Press, 1966.

Brooke, George, III. *With the First City Troop on the Mexican Border*. Philadelphia: John C. Winston Co., 1917.

Brownlow, Kevin. *The War, the West, and the Wilderness*. New York: Knopf, 1974.

Carman, Michael D. *United States Customs and the Madero Revolution*. El Paso: Texas Western Press, 1976.

Case, Alden Buell. *Thirty Years with the Mexicans in Peace and Revolution*. New York: Fleming H. Revell Co., 1917.

Clendenen, Clarence C. *Blood on the Border: The United States Army and the Mexican Irregulars*. New York: Macmillan, 1969.

———. *The United States and Pancho Villa: A Study in Unconventional Diplomacy*. Ithaca, N.Y.: Cornell University Press, 1961.

Coerver, Don M., and Linda B. Hall. *Texas and the Mexican Revolution: A Study in State and National Border Policy, 1910–1920*. San Antonio: Trinity University Press, 1984.

Crad, Joseph. *I Had Nine Lives: Fighting for Cash in Mexico and Nicaragua*. London: Sampson Low, Marston and Co., [1938].

Craighill, Edley. *The Musketeers*. Lynchburg, Va.: J. P. Bell Co., 1931.

Cumberland, Charles C. *Mexican Revolution: The Constitutionalist Years.* Austin: University of Texas Press, 1972.

Cutchins, John A. *A Famous Command: The Richmond Light Infantry Blues.* Richmond: Garrett and Massie, 1934.

Davis, John L. *The Texas Rangers: Their First 150 Years.* San Antonio: University of Texas at San Antonio, 1975.

Devlin, Thomas F. *Days of Discord: A Brief Chronology of the Mexican Revolution, 1910–1920.* El Paso, Tex.: American Printing Company, 1974.

Dos Passos, John. *Mr. Wilson's War.* New York: Doubleday and Co., 1962.

Evans, Eric J., and Jeffrey Richards. *A Social History of Britain in Postcards, 1870–1930.* London: Longmans, 1980.

Finnegan, John Patrick. *Against the Specter of a Dragon: The Campaign for American Military Preparedness, 1914–1917.* Westport, Conn.: Greenwood Press, 1974.

García, Mario T. *Desert Immigrants: The Mexicans of El Paso, 1880–1920.* New Haven: Yale University Press, 1981.

Geraci, Philip C. *Photojournalism: Making Pictures for Publication.* 2nd ed. Dubuque, Iowa: Kendall/Hunt Publishing Company, 1980.

Gibbons, Floyd P. *How the Laconia Sank: The Militia Mobilization on the Mexican Border.* Chicago: Daughaday and Company, 1917.

Gilderhus, Mark T. *Diplomacy and Revolution: U.S.-Mexican Relations under Wilson and Carranza.* Tucson: University of Arizona Press, 1977.

Gilpatrick, Rose A. "Old Loudon Hill," in *Historic Hallowell,* edited by Katherine H. Snell and Vincent P. Ledew. Hallowell, Maine: Hallowell Bicentennial Committee, 1972.

Goldhurst, Richard. *Pipeclay and Drill: John J. Pershing, The Classic American Soldier.* New York: Reader's Digest Press, 1977.

Gould, Lewis L., and Richard Greffe. *Photojournalist: The Career of Jimmy Hare.* Austin: University of Texas Press, 1977.

Gow, Lt. Kenneth. *Letters of a Soldier.* New York: Herbert B. Covert, [1920].

Grieb, Kenneth J. *The United States and Huerta.* Lincoln: University of Nebraska Press, 1969.

Haley, P. Edward. *Revolution and Intervention: The Diplomacy of Taft and Wilson with Mexico.* Cambridge, Mass.: Massachusetts Institute of Technology Press, 1970.

Hart, John M. *Revolutionary Mexico: The Coming and Process of the Mexican Revolution.* Berkeley: University of California Press, 1987.

Hersey, Mark L., ed. *Organization of the U.S. Naval Forces on Shore at Vera Cruz, Mexico, April 21–30, 1914.* Press of the U.S.S. *New Jersey,* 1914.

Hill, Jim Dan. *The Minute Man in Peace and War: A History of the National Guard.* Harrisburg, Pa.: The Stackpole Company, 1964.

Hill, Larry D. *Emissaries to a Revolution: Woodrow Wilson's Executive Agents in Mexico.* Baton Rouge: Louisiana State University Press, 1974.

Information Please Almanac, Atlas and Yearbook: 1970. New York: Dan Golenpaul Associates, 1969.

Katz, Friedrich. *The Secret War in Mexico: Europe, the United States and the Mexican Revolution.* Chicago: University of Chicago Press, 1981.

Kunz, Jeffrey R. M., ed. *The American Medical Association Family Medical Guide.* New York: Random House, 1982.

Lane, Jack C. *Armed Progressive: General Leonard Wood.* San Rafael, Calif.: Presidio Press, 1978.

Lay, Shawn. *War, Revolution, and the Ku Klux Klan:*

A Study of Intolerance in a Border City. El Paso: Texas Western Press, 1985.

Lewis, Betty. *Monterey Bay Yesterday: A Nostalgic Era in Postcards.* Fresno, Calif.: Valley Publishers, 1977.

Lewis, Tracey Hammond. *Along the Rio Grand.* New York: Lewis Publishing Company, 1916.

Lovell, S. D. *The Presidential Election of 1916.* Carbondale: Southern Illinois University Press, 1980.

Martínez, Andrea. *La Intervención norteamericana: Veracruz, 1914.* México: Secretaría de Educación Pública, 1982.

Martínez, Oscar J. *Border Boom Town: Ciudad Juárez Since 1848.* Austin: University of Texas Press, 1978.

———. *Fragments of the Mexican Revolution: Personal Accounts from the Border.* Albuquerque: University of New Mexico Press, 1983.

Mason, Herbert Mulloy, Jr. *The Great Pursuit.* New York: Random House, 1970.

McCulloch, Lou W. *Card Photographs: A Guide to Their History and Value.* Exton, Pa.: Schiffer Publishing, Ltd., 1981.

Meggs, Brown. *The War Train: A Novel of 1916.* New York: Atheneum, 1981.

Metz, Leon C. *Fort Bliss: An Illustrated History.* El Paso: Mangan Books, 1981.

Meyer, Michael C. *Huerta: A Political Portrait.* Lincoln: University of Nebraska Press, 1972.

———. *Mexican Rebel: Pascual Orozco and the Mexican Revolution.* Lincoln: University of Nebraska Press, 1967.

Millett, Allan R., and Peter Maslowski. *For the Common Defense: A Military History of the USA.* New York: Free Press, 1984.

Morgan, Hal, and Andreas Brown. *Prairie Fires and Paper Moons: The American Photographic Postcard: 1900–1920.* Boston: David R. Godine, 1981.

Newhall, Beaumont. *The History of Photography from 1839 to the Present Day.* New York: The Museum of Modern Art, 1964.

O'Reilly, Major Edward S. *Roving and Fighting: Adventures under Four Flags.* London: T. Werner Laurie Ltd., 1918.

Paine, Richard P. *The All-American Cameras: A Review of Graflex.* Houston, Tex.: Alpha Publishing Company, 1981.

Pershing, John J. *My Experiences in the World War.* 2 vols. New York: Frederick A. Stokes, 1931.

Pierce, Frank Cushman. *A Brief History of the Lower Rio Grande Valley.* Menasha, Wis.: George Banta Publishing Co., 1917.

Portilla, Santiago. *Madero de Ciudad Juárez a la Ciudad de México.* México: Secretaría de Educación Pública, 1983.

Previte, Joseph J. *Human Physiology.* New York: McGraw-Hill Book Company, 1983.

Quirk, Robert E. *An Affair of Honor: Woodrow Wilson and the Occupation of Veracruz.* New York: W. W. Norton, 1962.

Raat, William D. *Revoltosos: Mexico's Rebels in the United States, 1903–1923.* College Station: Texas A & M Press, 1981.

Raht, Carlysle Graham. *The Romance of Davis Mountains and Big Bend Country.* Odessa, Tex.: Rathbooks Co., 1919.

Rodney, George Brydges. *As a Cavalryman Remembers.* Caldwell, Idaho: Caxton Printers Ltd., 1944.

Ross, Stanley R. *Francisco I. Madero: Apostle of Mexican Democracy.* New York: Columbia University Press, 1955.

Russell, Thomas H. *Mexico in Peace and War: A Narrative of Mexican History and Conditions from the Earliest Times to the Present Hour, including an Account of the Military Operations by the United States* at Vera Cruz in 1914 and the Causes that Led Thereto. Chicago: Reilly and Britton Syndicate, 1914.

Ryan, Dorothy B. *Picture Postcards in the United States, 1893–1918*. 1st ed., rev. New York: Clarkson N. Potter, 1982.

Scott, Hugh L. *Some Memories of a Soldier*. New York: Century Co., 1928.

Smithers, W. D. *Chronicles of the Big Bend: A Photographic Memoir of Life on the Border*. Austin, Tex.: Madrona Press, 1976.

Smythe, Donald. *Guerrilla Warrior: The Early Life of John J. Pershing*. New York: Scribner, 1973.

Staff, Frank. *The Picture Postcard and Its Origins*. New York: Frederick A. Praeger, 1966.

Stark, Sam. "Keepsakes Series: Number One in a Series of Keepsakes." *West Coast Expositions and Galas*. San Francisco: The Book Club of California, 1970.

Strickler, Daniel B. *The Memoirs of Lieutenant Governor, Lieutenant General Daniel Bursk Strickler*. Lancaster, Pa.: [n.p.], 1932.

Sweetman, Jack. *The Landing at Vera Cruz: 1914*. Annapolis, Md.: United States Naval Institute, 1968.

Tompkins, Col. Frank. *Chasing Villa: The Story Behind the Story of Pershing's Expedition into Mexico*. Harrisburg, Pa.: Military Service Publishing Co., 1934.

Toulmin, Harry A. *With Pershing in Mexico*. Harrisburg, Pa.: Military Service Publishing Co., 1935.

Tyler, Ronnie C. *The Big Bend: A History of the Last Texas Frontier*. Washington, D.C.: National Park Service, U.S. Department of Commerce, 1975.

Vanderwood, Paul J. *Disorder and Progress: Bandits, Police and Mexican Development*. Lincoln: University of Nebraska Press, 1981.

Williams, Vernon. *Lieutenant Patton and the American Army in the Mexican Expedition, 1915–1916*. Austin: Presidial Press, 1983.

Woodcock, A. W. W. *Golden Days*. [n.p.], 1951.

II. Articles

Barry, Kitty. "Pitching Camp for Twenty-Thousand: An Observer's Impression of the Arrival of Our Troops in Texas." *Harper's Weekly* (April 1, 1911): 9ff.

Beckett, C. Tucker. "Military Photography in Mexico." *The Camera* (November 1916): 599–616.

Coerver, Don M., and Linda B. Hall. "The Arizona-Sonora Border in the Mexican Revolution, 1910–1920." *Journal of the West* 24 (April 1985): 75–87.

Collins, Peter, "War Nurtured Postcards: UPU Organizer Influenced Their Early Development." *Stamp Collector* (November 11, 1985): 10–11, 15.

Davis, Ed. "Collecting 'Old Auto' Postcards." *Postcard Collector* (March 1985): 50.

Fitch, George. "Upon the Threatened Extinction of the Art of Letter Writing." *American Magazine* (June 1910): 172–75.

Gannaway, Thomas D. "One Hundred and Forty-Four Postal Cards per Second: A New Machine for the Public Printer." *Scientific American* (July 1, 1911): 5.

Griswold del Castillo, Richard. "The Discredited Revolution: The Magonista Capture of Tijuana in 1911." *Journal of San Diego History* 26 (Fall 1980): 256–73.

Hall, Linda B. "The Mexican Revolution and the Crisis in Naco, 1914–1915." *Journal of the West* 16 (October 1977): 27–35.

Harris, Charles H., and Louis R. Sadler. "Pancho Villa and the Columbus Raid: The Missing Documents." *New Mexico Historical Review* 50 (October 1975): 335–46.

———. "The Plan of San Diego and the Mexican–

United States War Crisis of 1916: A Reexamination." *Hispanic American Historical Review* 58 (August 1978): 381–408.

———. "The Underside of the Mexican Revolution: El Paso, 1912." *The Americas* 39 (July 1982): 69–82.

Harris, Jodie P. "Protecting the Big Bend—A Guardsman's View." *Southwestern Historical Quarterly* 78 (January 1975): 292–302.

Henschen, Sigmund. "The Collapse of Our Militia: Showing How Our Volunteer System Works." *Forum* 56 (September 1916): 244–303.

Hutchinson, Rollin W., Jr. "The Motor Versus the Mule in Uncle Sam's War Department." *American Review of Reviews* 48 (July 1913): 59–64.

Katz, Frederich. "Pancho Villa and the Attack on Columbus, New Mexico." *American Historical Review* 83 (February 1978): 101–30.

La France, David G. "Francisco I. Madero and the 1911 Interim Governorship in Puebla." *The Americas* 42 (January 1986): 311–31.

"The Motor Truck in Peace and War," *Collier's* (January 8, 1916): 43–55.

Munch, Francis J. "Villa's Columbus Raid: Practical Politics or German Design?" *New Mexico Historical Review* 4 (July 1969): 189–214.

"Our Motor-Truck Railway." *Literary Digest* (May 20, 1916): 1488.

"Our Unpreparedness Revealed by Villa." *Literary Digest* (April 1, 1916): 883–86.

Polese, Richard, ed. "Assignment: Villa Raid, Excerpts from the Journal of Harold Palmer Brown." *El Palacio: Magazine of the Museum of New Mexico* (Fall 1980): 2–14.

Pratt, Walter Merriam. "On the Border with Our Army." *New England Magazine* 46 (July–August 1911): 30–38.

Randolf, J. Ralph. "Border Reaction to the Villa

Raids." *West Texas Historical Association Year Book* 49 (1973): 12–13.

Reid, Frederick. "Mobilizing the Flintlock Army–An Object Lesson. *Sunset* (May 1916): 16–18.

Sarber, Mary A. "W. H. Horne and the Mexican War Photo Postcard Company." *Password* 31 (Spring 1986): 5–15.

Tate, Michael L. "Pershing's Punitive Expedition: Pursuer of Bandits or Presidential Panacea?" *The Americas* 32 (July 1975): 46–72.

Turner, Virginia. "Photographer Leaves Priceless El Paso Heritage." *El Paso Herald Post* (January 8, 1985).

III. Documents, Unpublished Manuscripts, and Interviews

Beckett, C. Tucker. "Albums: C. Tucker Beckett's Photographs of the Mexican Expedition, U.S. Army 1916." National Archives of the United States, Still Pictures Branch, Record Group 165-CB.

Beecher, Dale F. "Incentive to Violence: Political Exploitations of Lawlessness on the United States–Mexico Border, 1866–1886." Ph.D. dissertation, University of Utah, 1982.

Cary, Norman M. "The Use of the Motor Vehicle in the U.S. Army." Ph.D. dissertation, University of Georgia, 1980.

Chynoweth, B. G. "Personal Recollections," dated October 24, 1967. History Research Collection, U.S. Army War College, Carlisle Barracks, Pa.

Coerver, Don M., and Linda B. Hall. "The Refuge: Mexican Migration to the United States, 1910–1920." Article in preparation by the authors.

Condax, Philip L., and Andrew F. Eskind. Private interview held at International Museum of Photography at George Eastman House, Rochester, N.Y., June 7, 1985.

El Paso Public Library, W. H. Horne Letter File; W. H. Horne Postcard File.

Halsted, Laurence. "Personal Recollections," dated September 1974. History Research Collection, U.S. Army War College, Carlisle Barracks, Pa.

Hardman, John O. Private interview, Warren, Ohio, September 12, 1985.

Harris, Charles H., and Louis R. Sadler. "United States Government Archives and the Mexican Revolution: Some New Approaches." Paper presented at the meeting of the American Historical Association, 1982, Washington, D.C.

Johnson, Robert Bruce. "The Punitive Expedition: A Military Diplomatic and Political History of Pershing's Chase after Pancho Villa, 1916–1917." Ph.D. dissertation, University of Southern California, 1964.

LaFrance, David G. "A People Betrayed: Francisco I. Madero and the Mexican Revolution in Puebla." Ph.D. dissertation, University of Indiana, 1984.

Monticone, Joseph Raymond. "Revolutionary Mexico and the U.S. Southwest: The Columbus Raid." M.A. thesis, California State University, Fullerton, 1981.

National Archives of the United States, Still Pictures Branch, Record Group 165-MP.

Rocha, Rodolfo, "The Influence of the Mexican Revolution of the Mexico-Texas Border, 1910–1916." Ph.D. dissertation, Texas Tech University, 1981.

Sandos, James A. "The Mexican Revolution and the United States, 1915–1917: The Impact of the Conflict in the Tamaulipas-Texas Frontier Upon the Emergence of Revolutionary Government in Mexico." Ph.D. dissertation, University of California, Berkeley, 1978.

IV. Newspapers and Magazines

American Review of Reviews (1911–16).
Border Work (Army YMCA with the Troops in Texas) (1916).
Collier's (1911–16).
El Correo de Chihuahua (1915–16).
Forum (1915–16).
Harper's Weekly (1911–16).
Kennebec Journal (1921).
Kodak Trade Journal (1910).
Literary Digest (1911–16).
Moving Picture World (1911–16).
New York Times (1911–17).
Outlook (1915–16).
El Paso Herald (1916).
El Paso Morning Times (1911–17, 1921).
San Antonio Light (1911–17).
Sunset (1915–16).
The World's Work (1911–16).

V. Sources of Postcards

Arizona Historical Society, Tucson, Ariz.
Ralph Bowman Collection, San Diego, Calif.
Andreas Brown Collection, New York City, N.Y.
Ralph Downey Collection, San Diego, Calif.
Murney Gurlach Collection, San Diego, Calif.
Nita Stewart Haley Memorial Library, Midland, Tex.
John Hardman Collection, Warren, Ohio.
Kansas State Historical Society, Topeka, Kans.
Library of Congress of the United States, Washington, D.C.
Edward McBride Collection, San Diego, Calif.
New Mexico State University, Library Special Collections, Las Cruces, N. Mex.

El Paso Public Library.
Pimería Alta Historical Society, Nogales, Ariz.
Carter Rila Collection, Gaithersburg, Md.
D. J. Sobery Collection, Decatur, Georgia.
Samuel Stark Collection, Pebble Beach, Calif.
Sul Ross State University, Library Special Collections,
    Alpine, Tex.
San Diego Historical Society.
University of Arizona, Library Special Collections,
    Tucson, Ariz.
University of California, Los Angeles, Research
    Library Special Collections.
U.S. Library of Congress, Washington, D.C.

Index

United States Marines, 119–20, 147
United States Navy, 10, 25, 26, 27, 118–19, 146,
    147, 148, 151, 152, 154, 155, 156, 157, 158
U.S.S. *Florida,* 119
U.S.S. *Louisiana,* 119
U.S.S. *Minnesota,* 27
U.S.S. *New Jersey,* 10, 26

Valle, Javier J., 68, 94
Vásquez Gómez, Emilio, 115, 127
vending machines, 7
Veracruz, Mexico, 10, 24, 66, 71, 118–20, 147, 160;
    cards of, 20, 21, 22, 25, 26, 27, 144, 145, 146,
    149, 151, 152, 153, 154, 155, 156, 158
Verhoeks, James J., 194, 232
Villa Ahumada, Mexico, 191
Villagrán, Rafael T., 79
Villa, Pancho, 10, 11, 12, 14, 28, 68, 71, 115, 117,
    120, 121, 123, 139, 173, 177, 178, 179–84, 186,
    196, 205, 251; cards of, 33, 34, 61, 77, 127, 161,
    200, 266
Villistas, 11, 57, 95, 99, 116, 177, 179–84, 244

W. M. Prilay Post Card Company, 10, 20
Washington Post, 121
war stories, 227

"watchful waiting," 199, 219
Wegeforth, Harry M., 138
White, B. T., 242
whorehouse, Pershing's, 190, 209
Wilson, Henry Lane, 116
Wilson, Woodrow, 10, 11, 14, 69, 116–18, 151, 182,
    184, 186, 191, 196–97
Wilson administration, 120, 122–23, 183, 184, 199,
    219
wireless equipment, 190, 251
Wisconsin, 236
woodcuts, 2
World Herald (Omaha), 183
World's Columbian Exposition, 2
World War I, 7, 8, 73, 136, 186, 193, 249, 254;
    preparedness for, 117, 186–90, 192, 236, 248
writing habits, 7
Wyoming, 112

Yaqui Indians, 265
Young Men's Christian Association (YMCA), 12, 52,
    53, 69, 194, 223

Zapata, Emiliano, 115, 117, 120, 121
Zapatistas, 116